Starkweather

Starkweather

The Story of a Mass Murderer

WILLIAM ALLEN

Illustrated with Photographs

Houghton Mifflin Company
<small>BOSTON</small> 1976

364.15
A

Library of Congress Cataloging in Publication Data

Allen, William, date
    Starkweather : the story of a mass murderer.

    1. Starkweather, Charles. 2. Murder—Nebraska.
I. Title.   1938 -1959
HV6248.S6274A44   364.1'523'0924 [B]   75-42125
ISBN 0-395-24077-8
Printed in the United States of America

V 10 9 8 7 6 5 4 3 2 1

FOR ANNA BELLE

ILLUSTRATIONS

following page 86

(The photos reproduced here, unless otherwise noted, are the property of the Journal-Star Printing Company of Lincoln, Nebraska, and are not to be reused without permission of the Journal-Star Printing Company.)

Starkweather

PROLOGUE

In January 1958, a nineteen-year-old Nebraskan, Charles Raymond Starkweather, accompanied and possibly assisted by his fourteen-year-old girlfriend, Caril Ann Fugate, murdered ten people in eight days. After their capture, Starkweather confessed to having committed another murder the previous month. Newspapers and magazines said that it was the second worst case of multiple murder in United States history, topped only by Howard Unruh, a deranged ex-serviceman who in 1949 shot and killed thirteen people in Camden, New Jersey. Because Unruh was shown to be berserk, and because such acts were unheard of in modern times, he was thought of as an anomaly. Charlie and Caril could not be so easily delineated. They were not obviously insane and neither had a police record more serious than a traffic violation. Though it was suspected that Charlie had a mental disorder which made him prone to violence, the disorder was not immediately defined. And in

1

other ways he and Caril seemed disturbingly close to being like other young couples of the time.

The Nebraska murders marked the beginning of a trend toward increased violence on the part of individuals acting in relative autonomy in his country. Examples of multiple murderers are much easier to list now than in 1958 — the names Speck, Whitman, De Salvo, Corll, Manson come immediately to mind, and there are others. And it may be significant that almost all of them spent at least a portion of their adolescence in the fifties. Killers may follow patterns but they also may be as individual as fingerprints. We can put them in broad categories, call them "antisocial" or "sociopathic," but such terms, intended to make for easier understanding, may instead limit our reach. A psychologist at Charlie's trial made an appropriate analogy. He said that you can catalogue or categorize books all you want, but in order to know what's inside one you have to open it and read it.

Charlie could have lived and killed in any time in history, but he didn't. He lived in the fifties and in part it was the social pressures of that time that triggered his actions. Like his more acceptable Hollywood counterpart James Dean, he became to many a symbol of the rebel teen-ager. He literally represented only those who found their ways to prisons and asylums, but it is true that what some of the rest of us coming of age then fantasized and repressed, he acted out in a pattern so terrible it may never be forgotten — and probably it shouldn't be, in the way that the patterns of wars and tornadoes shouldn't be forgotten. He may not have been one of us — Charlie was hopelessly disjunct from all humanity — but he looked like us and he made real our most fearful dreams.

I was seventeen, a senior in high school, when the Starkweather murders took place, and while working on this book, I recalled many of my own experiences during that period. The more I remembered of what happened — or came within a hair's breadth of happening — the less broad seemed the gulf between Charlie Starkweather and the rest of us. In Dallas, Texas, a city with enough violence for a dozen Lincoln, Nebraskas, and in particular my school and neighborhood on the south side, individuality and status were commonly determined by brute force. Fist fights, knife fights, gang fights — the south side had them all. They didn't happen everyday but were always in the wings, anticipated to the point where some boys kept hands curled into fists whenever they walked the halls between classes. I was acquainted with boys who carried great push-button stilettos which would clack open with such force it took a trained hand just to hold onto them. Some carried zip guns and pistols to school. Richard Speck, who went to Chicago and killed seven student nurses, became the most infamous from among our south side ranks. I was witness to several stabbings and a shooting at the Texas Theater, where Oswald was later apprehended. One boy attending South Oak Cliff carried a sawed-off shotgun in his car and occasionally used it to blast cars whose drivers were trying to drag-race with him. Gangs with names like the Lakewood Rats and the Jim Town Gang fought with chains and jagged beer cans on the grassy banks of the Trinity River, where Bonnie and Clyde first met. Thievery and vandalism were common, often done on dares. One boy from Sunset High School stole a new Corvette for a joy ride, then plunged it into nearby Mountain Creek Lake, jumping out at the last second à la *Rebel Without a Cause*. Drag races and playing chicken with one another in cars were daily events. Some would drive out on Highway 77 and challenge the semis. Almost everybody drove recklessly; I earned enough speeding tickets during my senior year to inspire me to flee into the arms of the army two weeks after graduation.

Adolescence has long been thought of as a difficult time for

3

most people, a time of erratic and violence-prone activity, and it may be that the fifties were no worse in that regard than any other decade. But at least they seemed worse because teen-agers were given so much attention and therefore definition by the news and entertainment media. Of course, not everybody rebelled. In Dallas, there was still a clean-cut majority who made A's in physics, respected their parents, belonged to ROTC, and became class presidents — they got through those years without risking being shot, stabbed, maimed in a car wreck, or going to prison. With their short hair and button-down sport shirts, they played it safe, kept a low profile, avoided the destructive force that had snagged the hoodlum few.

Who decided who conformed and who didn't? Each of us individually, it might appear, but there didn't seem to be much choice at the time. The serious rebel, headed eventually for a life of crime, was painfully aware of the social and economic pressures which made him unable or unwilling to compete for grades and an acceptable social standing. He was also aware of oppressive parents who sometimes tried to make him live by different standards of morality than they did themselves — and he often lashed out against them. But he usually directed his frustration against others his own age before he turned it against society at large.

There was another large group, often from poor but honest and hardworking families, caught somewhere between conformity and rebellion. Many of us, sometimes against our better judgment, felt compelled to at least play the role of rebels. The convenient symbols of powers, the emphasis on style, the comfortable group identification, all had a primitive appeal that we simply couldn't resist. Our parents, though perhaps decent and well-intentioned people, had not raised us to resist it. Or perhaps they had, and we failed them.

Teen-agers in Lincoln then were held more in check than in

Dallas, but they expressed the same tendencies. Tracy Kontos, today an employee in the Lancaster County sheriff's office in Lincoln, was a teen-ager during the Starkweather murder spree. She reflects: "I was considered a rebel, which shows you how really conservative and intolerant of youth Lincoln was back then. I did things like wear make-up a year younger than other girls. I used profanity. I dated a boy who went to another high school than I did. That was unheard of. And he had side-burns, God forbid. They didn't even come to the bottom of his ears but they meant he was a hood. He turned out better than most of my friends, went through college, and became a deputy sheriff. A hood in those days was somebody who stole hubcaps and got into fights for reasons of status. The other kids admired him for it too — it showed nerve. But Charlie was another matter entirely. What he did was sick."

My teen-age days were more style than substance. My friends and I realized at an early age the power and status of having an automobile, and I worked hard and saved my money to buy one. Within weeks after I got my 1953 Ford, it was shaved hood and deck, lowered in back, had pinstripes, twin glass-pack mufflers, skirts, Oldsmobile taillights, and a rolled and pleated interior. It was one of the better-looking cars at South Oak Cliff and, by doing things like occasionally skipping school and racking my pipes outside the classroom windows, I built an identity around it. Just as my car looked good but wasn't "hot," I spent more of my energy trying to look cool rather than being tough. We were all fanatics about our hair, working on it in the school restrooms until our arms grew weak. I plastered mine with Brylcreem and combed it in a weird, complicated style that Charlie himself often wore. I can't tell you where the aesthetic sense came from that developed that hairdo, but it was absolute and I was in accord with it. Using my comb and both hands, I would work till I was ready to

5

collapse — then finally it would be just right, a work of art. During those days I walked around like I had a book on my head, and was a master at avoiding areas likely to generate sudden gusts of wind.

But violence was still a necessary, integral part of being even a pseudorebel. Most of us hated the reality of it, and we got in only enough fights to maintain our dignity. But we loved the idea of violence. One time some of us faked a gang fight with knives across from a junior high school and became legend to a hundred pubescent children. We could go over Roller Coaster Hill at ninety miles an hour with aplomb. It was a cheap thrill as long as we didn't crash, and we knew we wouldn't do that; it was like going into battle — the other guy may get it but not us. We even once went through a mad-bomber stage and tried to blow up a wooden bridge on a country road on the outskirts of town. The explosion made a sound like thunder but the bridge didn't budge: it was style without substance.

But our fantasies, at least, came close to matching even Starkweather's. A few of us often talked of stealing a jet plane from the nearby Naval Air Station, taking it up to 40,000 feet, and diving into the center of downtown Dallas. We thought that would show the bastards (the world at large) and we could make history at the same time. Nobody would ever forget the day the kids wiped out Big D. It would be necessary to sacrifice ourselves, but that didn't matter. We would be out of the rat race, and we believed in reincarnation then, anyway. It would give us a chance to test the accuracy of our Bible, *The Search for Bridey Murphy*. The thing that stopped us, of course, was we didn't know how to fly.

That fantasy was distant enough from reality to be safe, but others weren't. One time we were out at a local rock quarry, shooting bottles with .22s. There was a small airport nearby, and a light plane came in low over the quarry on a landing approach. Almost casually, we pointed our rifles upward and took a few pot shots. Nothing happened, the plane flew on, but I was deeply disturbed by the incident later. To us, that hadn't been a human being up there, it had been more like shooting at a bird, or perhaps acting out a scene in a war movie. For just a moment, our fantasies had blurred into reality: if we had been better shots it might have been irrevocable.

Most of my friends and I graduated from high school, barely, and went on to the service, to work, or to college. By the time I got to college, after three years in the army, the old high school days seemed like a nightmare. Except for basic training, it had been the worst time of my life. Adolescence is a period when we find identities for ourselves, but we need guides and models, and in retrospect I could see that the options my friends and I had were few. Most of our parents had limited horizons — mine wanted me to drop out of high school and have a career in the air force — our neighborhood was poor and culturally impoverished, our school was like a prison and the teachers guards. Some of us very nearly took the easiest option the fifties offered, and I have wondered why we didn't. It might have been because our families, despite being perhaps poor and uneducated, were good people who cared about us. I considered my family puritanical and unreasonable when I was a teenager, but their values had been instilled in me as a child and I eventually returned to many of them. I wondered what would have happened if they had been criminals? If they had resented me? If I had been a subject of ridicule because I was born bowlegged, half-blind, with a speech impediment, and dumb?

Chapter ONE

DURING THE LAST MONTHS of Charlie Starkweather's life, while he awaited his execution in 1959, he frequently was visited by the prison chaplain, his family — particularly his mother — and by Dr. James M. Reinhardt, a professor of criminology at the University of Nebraska. Others who visited with him were Deputy Warden John Greenholtz and Lincoln *Journal* reporter Marjorie Marlette — who was the only other writer besides Reinhardt to see Charlie in prison. Also, Charlie was quite close to Mike Shimerda, one of the prison guards outside his cell. Those were the principal people who knew Charlie in his final days, and their views of him differ considerably.

Reinhardt previously had written accounts of unusual murder cases and now was preparing a criminology text, *The Murderous Trail of Charles Starkweather.* According to others who saw them together, the two men did not always get along. Charlie often was resistant to Reinhardt's probes, preferring lighter con-

9

versation with his family and guard Mike Shimerda. Also, Charlie was writing a book himself — his life's story — and could not understand how anyone could tell his story better than he could. As it turned out, Charlie's book was never published, but after his death sections of it appeared in Reinhardt's text.

Charlie was uneven and inconsistent in his writing, which was a characteristic of his personality and intelligence in general. He could not spell or punctuate, and seldom wrote a correct sentence, and his concepts were often childishly naive. But at times he had rather sophisticated insights and, because of his intensity and associative ability with language, he could command real narrative power. He had such problems with spelling and malapropisms that his writing sometimes defies word-by-word explication — yet he still managed to communicate on a less precise level. Also, he used a dictionary in prison and seems to have experimented with new words with only qualified success.

Marjorie Marlette, who helped negotiate the sale of part of his book to *Parade* magazine, says, "Like many offenders, Charlie saw his book as a way of atoning, of making something good come out of the wrongs he committed. He wrote and rewrote and carefully copied each page — an extremely demanding job for someone with only a smattering of education. He just refused to let the mechanics of handwriting, the techniques of grammar and spelling, hold him back."

Referring to a talk he had to make as a child in front of a kindergarten class, Charlie wrote this passage — which later appeared in Reinhardt's book: ". . . I began to speak . . . my voice was smerying faint and cracked, the kids bursted into laughter . . . I flinch, startle, flaccid, lacking in firmness, then I was completely flabbergast as my words became flat as I started to speak again I sadden they had no regard for my feelings . . ."

Reinhardt wrote that Charlie was convinced his story would be read by millions. He wanted to know how soon it could be published, what kind of jacket it would have, how many pages it would make. He said he hoped to earn at least thirty thousand dollars in royalties. Reinhardt wrote that Charlie was very upset when told that publishers weren't interested in his manuscript — and he was furious when some editor at *Parade* underlined passages from the manuscript, despite the fact the magazine wanted to publish parts of the story. Charlie accused Reinhardt of ruining the book and even stealing a few pages of it.

Marlette, however, didn't see such egotism in Charlie. "He didn't like what *Parade* did to his writing," she says, "but neither did his family. Neither did I for that matter. It was edited to the point it became flat. And as far as Charlie thinking his book would be read by millions, I seriously doubt it. He must have been kidding Reinhardt when he said that. Or responding to a suggestion made by Reinhardt. I always felt that Charlie was experiencing remorse so deep and hopeless that he felt he might as well go along with Reinhardt's perceptions of him as not. It seemed to me that Charlie was reacting to leads the criminologist gave him, rather than expressing his own feelings."

Though Charlie talked openly to others — including psychologist Charles Munson who spent a total of eighteen hours with him and asked many personal questions — Reinhardt found him to be suspicious when asked about himself. Often he would refuse to answer even the simplest question until it was asked in several different ways. According to Marlette, Reinhardt occasionally would ask embarrassing questions in an attempt to anger Charlie and elicit a response that way. Yet, in more casual conversation Charlie sometimes would speak freely. Reinhardt wrote that he enjoyed talking about what a good shot he was, memories from his childhood, his late night walks, and the almost visionary things he sometimes saw, heard, and said.

From the difficult interviews, and from Charlie's own writing, the material emerged which Reinhardt shaped into a portrait of the rebel teen-age killer of the 1950s. After seventeen years, with both men now dead, it is difficult to say how well the professor rendered his material, but nevertheless his observations provide a glimpse of Charlie that cannot be ignored.

Reinhardt suggested that Charlie had fantasies of killing all the people on earth and then living in peace with the animals. Charlie believed, wrote Reinhardt, that though he walked among men he did not belong to their world. The world of men to him was symbolized by the expensive Cornhusker Hotel restaurant in which others sat and ate fine food while he could only stand outside in the cold Nebraska wind and gaze through the window. It made him hate the whole world for making him what he was.

In his life's story, Charlie wrote that some people believe this is a wonderful world, but if it was he had never experienced it. He said the best things in life had been denied him: he had never been to Los Angeles or New York City, never eaten in a fine restaurant, never seen the New York Yankees play. It seemed to him, according to Reinhardt, that if he could be rid of people then he could be rid of the hatred inside him which never went away or diminished but had grown more intense over the years until he was crazy from it. Then perhaps he could walk in peace in a beautiful forest, with deer and rabbits, and watch the wonderful sunsets. If Charlie had a world of his own, wrote Reinhardt, besides the fictional world of cowboy movies and comic books, it was the world of nature. Reinhardt quoted Charlie as writing, "I would set down against a large tree, and enjoy the scenery . . . The fallen trees lay in a frightful tangle, and over and about them grew the undergrowth, the tupical trees stood stern . . ." He went on to write that the trees seemed supernatural, and that between the jagged limbs and greenish-brown and yellow foliage he could see for miles and miles into the sky, into the undiscovered and the unknown. At such moments an irresistible feeling would sweep over his soul and, entering a dreamlike state, he somehow seemed to acquire new self-awareness. But something, an approaching animal or person, always would snap him back to reality. He said that his most enjoyable experiences were being alone in beautiful woods, where time seemed to be at a standstill.

In an article published in the Lincoln *Journal*, Marjorie Marlette wrote, ". . . the condemned man has spent a lot of time looking out of his one-barred window. From it the redhead who has always loved hunting, fishing, and the outdoors, can see the sky, a large patch of well-kept grass and flowers . . ." Marlette said that a line from a poem he wrote for his mother in his cell perhaps reflected his thoughts at those times: "The stranger asks no greater glory till life is through than to spend one last minute in wilderness."

During the interviews with Reinhardt, Charlie talked about the many evenings he spent in a beer joint in Lincoln. On those drunken evenings he said he often had fantasies of becoming a criminal, and on one of them it seems he plotted his first major crime. Apparently, his fourteen-year-old girlfriend, Caril, was a part of his plans from the beginning. By leading a life of crime he thought he could be free of their families, free of his job as a garbage collector, free of everyone who had ever looked down on him and called him names. For the first time he would have money for anything he wanted. He would have guns and wouldn't be afraid of using them if anybody stood in his way. Charlie told Reinhardt that up until then they hadn't done much out of the ordinary, but soon all the people who had laughed at him would have something interesting to talk about. He wasn't afraid of anything, and if it came to a show-down he wasn't afraid to die either. But he knew one thing: he wouldn't be the first to die.

Reinhardt wrote that Charlie thought that hauling garbage was work for a nincompoop, and the money came in too slowly. He needed a lot of money if he was going to keep Caril, and he knew there was a lot around for the taking if you weren't afraid to pick it up. He had wanted to become a criminal for a long time. He read detective comics by the dozens and watched anything on TV or at the movies with shooting in it. There was little he loved more than the feel of a gun in his hands, the sound of it being cocked, the sudden rush of a moving target, and the explosion. He loved to take guns apart and put them together, to oil and clean them. Despite his poor eyesight, he was a good shot, usually shooting from the hip rather than tak-ing careful aim. He knew guns better than anything, and now he thought it was time to make use of what he knew. People respected a gun. He thought Caril would like him even more for the way he could use it to get the things they wanted.

Charlie later told his prosecutors — County Attorney Elmer Scheele and Chief Deputy Dale Fahrnbruch — that he had wanted "to get out of town," but to do it he needed some money at the start. He had thought many times of a bank holdup, but the idea scared him. Finally he settled on the plan that would become his first major crime: he would rob the Crest gas station out on Cornhusker Highway, just north of town. From what he told authorities later, and from police interviews with the station attendants, it was learned that he used to hang out there, working on his car, making meals out of cold drinks and candy from the machines, and occasionally he had even slept in his car in the parking lot.

The night attendant, Robert McClung, had befriended him and always woke him when it was time for him to get up and collect garbage. McClung had recently changed jobs and Charlie hardly knew the new attendant, Robert Colvert, but he knew the routine at the station. He knew when the attendants changed shifts, and he had hovered in the office and eyed the money as they counted it. He wouldn't have to case the place, wouldn't have to worry about something unexpected happening, and he had learned from his comic books that after this type of crime the police wouldn't be looking very hard for a local person. They would be after a transient headed on down the highway. All he had to do was wear a disguise so the attendant couldn't recognize him — and if Colvert did recognize him, that would be Colvert's tough luck.

Charlie once told Reinhardt that as he walked home from his favorite bar about the time he made these plans, the shadows from trees and bushes along the way had something to say to him. Sometimes before they had made fun of him and called him a stupid coward. They had made him feel as though he were already a dead man who just hadn't been buried yet. But on this night they danced for him, as if he had just returned to life as a hero who was about to go into battle. He swaggered along the sidewalk, muttering that he wouldn't take any more shit.

Reinhardt asked him about that, wondering how the shadows had known he was coming just at that time. Charlie replied that Reinhardt must be trying to say he was crazy. He said that his experience with the shadows was no different than a child riding a stick horse and pretending it was real.

Home from the bar, he lay on the bed in his work clothes, with his hands behind his head. Until now it seemed that every day of his life had been a lost day which had taken a little piece of him. But that was over. Something told him that Caril was thinking about him now. She seemed to be asking if he was worth standing by, if he would really fight for her.

He began to drift off, then was awakened by a fragmented

dream — the sudden swerve of the car, the sound of flying bullets, and Caril's excited laughter. He continued the dream in his imagination and saw them shooting and killing with incredible fury, going out in a blaze of glory, while the hushed and frightened voices of everyone who had ever made fun of him now spoke in awe.

During one interview, Charlie told Reinhardt of a time in the early hours of the morning, before his brother came to pick him up to collect garbage, when he was visited by Death. It woke him — or did it? Maybe it came in a dream. But whether it was a dream or a vision, it was there outside the window, looking like part man, part bear. He could see it only from the waist up. It had no arms or ears, no neck, just a big chest that tapered upward to a small rounded head. But Death was his friend and had visited him many times before, sometimes in different forms. Often Death came as a whistling sound, close and loud at first, then mournful and low until it was gone. The dying sound of the whistle left him stricken, paralyzed, for several minutes. But he was not afraid. He knew the other side was better than this one. Sometimes after Death had visited him, he would go out in his car and drive the country roads at top speed, or play chicken with other boys who had cars. He never chickened out — he was giving Death a chance to take him if it was time. Once when he was on one of his high-speed drives he considered jerking the steering wheel and plunging his car into a gorge. But he didn't. If Death had wanted any help it would have told him.

He had come to love Death, to the point he felt that nothing could come between it and himself. He told Reinhardt he had broken up with a girl because he was beginning to like her, and it was getting in the way with his pact with Death. Caril, though, didn't get in the way. She laughed when he talked about Death, said he was a crazy person, but she always promised to go with him all the way. A girl who was willing to die with him — it was too good to be true, yet there she was.

This time Death brought him a coffin and wanted him to get inside. He rose from the bed and seemed to float through the window and into the black box. Then Death sent the coffin sailing off to hell. The coffin flew until it came to a tremendous fire and the heat burned away the wood and left Charlie standing on a street with giant flames on either side. He had always thought that hell would be hot and that the flames would torture him for eternity but he was wrong. The flames were soothing and more beautiful than anything he had ever seen on earth. Then Charlie was back in his bed again. Now he knew more than ever that Death was his friend and that where he was going was better than here. But don't be in a hurry, Death seemed to tell him. Your time will come. And when it does, Caril will be with you.

The unusual name of Starkweather, with all its nuances, fit Charlie well, but it seems to be a misnomer for most other members of the relatively small Starkweather clan. The first Starkweather sailed to America in 1640 from the Isle of Man in the Irish Sea; since then the name has been honorable and even distinguished on local levels around the country. A school in Michigan, a town in North Dakota, streets in several cities, all have been named after various outstanding Starkweathers. Starkweathers, generally, have made reputations for themselves as civil servants and during time of war. There is no history of crime or insanity in the family.

The Lincoln, Nebraska, branch was poor and uneducated but, for the most part, regarded as hardworking and law-abiding. Charlie was born at the Starkweather home in Lincoln on November 24, 1938, to Guy and Helen Starkweather, both native Nebraskans. He was the third child in a family of seven boys and one girl.

On the surface, Charlie's early years do not appear to be much different from those of other children from similiar backgrounds. The family was poor but not impoverished — there was always enough to eat — and he did not miss affluence then because he had never known it. He had a father to teach him necessary skills, a mother to turn to when he needed her, and two older brothers to play with. Charlie remembered his preschool years as idyllic, one happy romp playing cowboys and Indians with his brothers, helping his mother with the canning, and going fishing with his father. Neighbors viewed the Starkweather family as close, the children well behaved.

There were problems at home, though, that would lead a psychiatrist at Charlie's trial to testify, "I think the family environment didn't teach him to be an ordinary person. I think the person he fears most is his father. I think he took out on other people some of his feelings he may have had toward his own family."

Guy Starkweather, a small and rather handsome man, talkative, characterized in the newspapers as "colorful," struck some people as perhaps best suited for clerical work in a store or office. But instead he had become a carpenter and jack-of-all-trades. He didn't have the necessary physical stamina and, because of various ailments including a weak back and arthritis, did not work regularly. Helen, a small woman with frizzy red hair, was described by those close to the Starkweathers as strong and kind, the one who held things together. Besides raising such a large family she had had to work as a waitress since 1946. Charlie, questioned about his home life after his arrest, always spoke highly of his mother, but was more reserved about his father. He indicated a need for the man's respect, but also seemed to have a deep-seated hostility.

Whatever idyllic memories a person may choose to recall of the time before he's five or six, the test of those years comes when he has to leave the self-contained family environment and make it in the outside world. He has either been prepared for it or he hasn't.

Charlie's first day of school was a disaster, and morbid memories of the day followed him obsessively for years. He found relief from them for the first time when his first victim lay dead on a country road outside Lincoln.

Charlie had a remarkable ability to recall unpleasant details from his past, and in his life's story he re-created almost minute by minute his experience at Saratoga Elementary School. He was five years old and entering kindergarten, which was in the same two-story red brick building as the elementary classes. His two older brothers, Rodney and Leonard, who were seven and nine and relatively successful in the world away from home, walked him to school and showed him to the right room. Charlie wrote that as he was walking to class all enjoyment and excitement left him and he began to tremble; not even his brothers' reassurances could make him stop shaking.

The teacher, whom Charlie remembered as a "Mrs. Mott," welcomed them, called the roll, made a little talk about the importance of discipline in their lives, and asked everyone to stand and put his hand on his breast and, Reinhardt quoted Charlie, ". . . reside . . . The Pledge Allegation To The Flag."

Then the children had to go before the class and talk about their hobbies or summer activities. As Charlie waited his turn he planned out his talk: He would tell about playing with his brothers, canning vegetables with his mother, going fishing, and going to the movies. Because of his name he was one of the last to be called. As he walked to the front of the room he thought he heard giggles, which made him more nervous than he already was. Charlie had a slight speech impediment, saying "wouse" instead of "house," which, combined with a further muddling of words, made the class laugh at his talk. Finally he became so confused and upset that the teacher told him to sit down.

After that, Charlie was sure the other children were staring at him and laughing behind his back. There was a little playhouse in the room, and later in the day he crawled in it to play with two other children. The children left. Reinhardt quoted Charlie: "I sat staring out the little door, glaring antagonists, pinoned, thus, strained toward the kids about the room . . . and it seems as though I could see my heart before my eyes, turning dark black with hate of rages, of harhequinade, stripped from that of munner life leaving only naked being-hate." Then he wrote that Mrs. Mott came over and falsely accused him of telling the other children they couldn't play in the house. She put him at a desk and told him to draw a picture for his mother. Charlie noticed right away that he was the only child sitting alone at a desk; all the others were happily playing together.

During recess, team leaders divided the class up to play a form of soccer. It happened that there was an uneven number of boys in the class and after the teams were divided Charlie was standing alone. One team leader hesitated, thinking he was going to have to choose the bowlegged runt, but Charlie wrote that Mrs. Mott "saved" the leader by having Charlie sit on the bench as a substitute in case someone got hurt.

Before the nightmarish day ended, the other children were either avoiding him or openly making fun of him, ridiculing his short bowed legs and red hair. He told himself that one day he would have his revenge. And he wanted revenge not only on the children but the whole world.

On the second day of school, Charlie got into his first fight. He enjoyed it.

Though Charlie was later found to be of average or even

slightly above average intelligence, he was considered dull-normal in school and drifted from year to year in slow-learner groups. He passed a grade whenever he began to get too big for the rest of the boys in the class. When he had trouble in the first grade, he quickly quit trying and never concentrated on his studies again. His biggest problem had been his eyesight — and the problem went undetected until he was fifteen. He was first tested and fitted for glasses in 1954 when a test showed him to be myopic, with a rating of 20–200. He could barely read the giant E on the optometrist's chart at twenty feet. At that distance he was, for practical purposes, blind. As a child, the blackboard at the front of the room had been little more than a rumor to him. His eyesight was one of a number of problems overlooked by his parents and teachers. Some would not be uncovered until the counsel for his defense took an interest in 1958.

But Charlie was good in gym. Despite his physical problems, he was fast, strong, coordinated, and performed gymnastic feats as well as anyone at the school. One day the gym teacher made him the official student gym assistant. It was a proud moment for Charlie, one of his few triumphs, but it also gave him a taste of power and he took advantage of it. Lancaster County sheriff Merle Karnopp's son, Dennis, was attending school with Charlie at the time. "Dennis was a little overweight then," Sheriff Karnopp recalls. "The day Charlie took over he strutted up to him, poked him in the stomach with his finger, and said, 'We're gonna have to take a little of that off you, fella.' "

Still, being a success in gym was hardly enough for Charlie, and he used his fighting ability to gain prestige and self-esteem. By the time he reached the ninth grade, the year he dropped out, he was having fights almost daily. In prison he wrote that he was like a hound looking for a fight and that he considered

21

everyone his enemy. He said that the other children picking on him and not being his friend caused him to have black moods — and that everyone knew to leave him alone whenever he was in one of these moods. These periods of melancholy stayed with him all of his life. He blamed all of his fights on being made fun of as a child. Sometimes his battles were brief outbursts of violence, but other times they were frenzied and prolonged, not ending until they were broken up or his opponent lay senseless. He earned a reputation for being one of the meanest, toughest kids in Lincoln — which got him into still more fights because there were always other boys around who wanted to say they could whip Charlie Starkweather.

For the ninth grade, he transferred from Irving to Everett Junior High where it was hoped he could make a better adjustment. There was another tough kid in his new class, Bob Von Busch, and it was obvious to both of them from the start that they were going to have to have it out. Bob was a stocky boy, much larger than Charlie, and wore his hair in a flattop with "wings" — long, swept-back hair on the sides. He was a year younger than Charlie but looked and acted older. The hostility between the two mounted until one day they went at each other right in the classroom. After wrecking the room, the fight spilled out into the hall where they beat each other until they both collapsed from exhaustion. Today, Bob, who drives a cement truck in Lincoln and runs the city's Moose Lodge, says, "For his size, Charlie was the roughest guy I ever fought. I'd say neither one of us won that fight — it was more like we both lost it."

Charlie and Bob became friends after the fight and palled around together for several years. Charlie had a small group of friends — mostly boys he had fought — and to this circle he was usually generous and amiable. "He could be the kindest person you've ever seen," Bob says. "He'd do anything for you if he liked you. He was a hell of a lot of fun to be around, too. Everything was just one big joke to him. But he had this other side. He could be mean as hell, cruel. If he saw some poor guy on the street who was bigger than he was, better looking, or better dressed, he'd try to take the poor bastard down to his size. But I didn't think too much about it at the time. We were all a little like that then. We all had a lot of growing up to do."

Charlie was closer to Bob than to the other friends, and as they became older they frequently double-dated, going to the movies, then cruising Runza's drive-in restaurant or the Dutch Mill drive-in. They avoided the more popular King's Food Host because of the prowl cars usually parked there. Sometimes they went out to Capital Beach auto track where Charlie raced a hot rod and had a daredevil reputation in the demolition derby event.

"For years," Bob says, "you never saw one of us without the other. As long as we stuck together, people pretty much left us alone. He even moved in with me and my old man for a while. That was when he was about sixteen, right after he had had a big fight with Guy. After that he was over at our place far more than he ever was at home." They went in together on a 1941 Ford and made beer runs to Kansas where they were able to buy 3.2 beer and then sell it for a profit to friends in Lincoln. They would swipe cars, usually for joy rides, but sometimes Charlie stripped them down to use the parts or sell them. "We were pretty wild," Bob says, "but mostly we were just out to have a good time. You know the movie *American Graffiti*? Remember when the kids yanked the rear end out from under the cop car? We did exactly the same thing to a patrol car one night — chained the rear axle to the Runza drive-in. When the cop car took off it moved the whole Runza off its foundation."

During those days Charlie was a fanatic about James Dean,

and he and Bob went together to see all of the actor's movies. "I guess you might say James Dean was Charlie's idol," Bob says. "He looked a lot like him and he acted like him. But Charlie acted like Dean before he had ever heard of the guy. That's why he liked him so much. All of a sudden here was somebody on the screen who was just like he was. Charlie never imitated Dean exactly, but he did get a few ideas from him — little things, mostly, like standing a certain way."

Charlie had almost mastered the James Dean look — the sleepy, surly expression with a cigarette hanging from slightly parted lips — and he liked to wear tight, low-riding blue jeans, cowboy boots, and a black motorcycle jacket with the collar turned up. Often he combed his dark red hair straight back like Dean's; other times he kept it oiled and combed in a more complicated coiffure: ducktails, sideburns, long hair combed up and pulled forward to culminate in front with two high pom-padoured curls. Though Charlie certainly bore a similiarity to Dean, his features did not have the same refinement; Charlie had a pug nose, his neck seemed almost too thick for his head, and he had freckles. The slope of his forehead, his thick eyebrows, his heavy jaw at times combined to give him an almost brutish look. And his full-length image was even more flawed: When he walked, his bowed legs caused him to move in a caricature of a cowboy's swagger, and he was only five-feet-five.

In 1956 Bob started dating a girl named Barbara Fugate from the Belmont section of Lincoln. One day he got Charlie to agree to go over to meet the girl's younger sister, Caril. The sister was barely thirteen, Bob told him, but she looked more like eighteen. The four wound up at the Nebraska Theater on a double date, and after that night Caril only had one date with another boy. When Charlie found out about it, he hunted the boy down and threatened to kill him if he saw her again. The boy never came back. Word spread that the two were going steady, and Charlie was no longer bothered with competition. "After that, it was the four of us running around together," Bob says. "We went to the movies a lot, the drive-ins mostly. It was all we were old enough to do. But these weren't hot dates at all. It was more like a bunch of kids just piling in the car and looking for a good time. Charlie was pretty young for his age. He wasn't much for making out at all. To tell the truth, I don't think he knew what to do with it. He talked about it a lot, but when it came down to doing anything I think he just got too excited. And Caril was awfully young too — she didn't know her way around nearly as well as people thought."

But Caril Fugate, barely a teen-ager, changed the course of Charlie's life. It is easy to understand why he was attracted to her. She was a perfect assimilation of the attitudes, fads, and fashions of the times — and she liked him. Caril was small but well developed for her age, wore her dark brown hair in a pony-tail, and enjoyed going around in jeans, majorette boots, and a man's shirt with the sleeves rolled up. She was thought of as "spunky" and of having "elfish charm," but she was also quick-tempered and rebellious. Some adults who knew her called her a "little snip." She hadn't been as sheltered as some other girls in her class, and this gave her an air of confidence that made her seem older. She used profanity that surprised even Charlie at times, and was driving a car years before most other girls in Lincoln. Reinhardt quoted Charlie as saying that he had never known such a young girl who knew so much. He felt that she acted like an adult, and this made him want to be with her.

But in other ways Caril was ignorant and backward for her age. She had failed a grade in elementary school and was con-sidered a slow learner. She didn't know the United States had been in the Korean war. She had heard of Harry Truman but couldn't identify him from a photograph. She had never trav-eled anywhere out of the state and, except for one short trip to the Sand Hills of Nebraska, had seldom been out of Lincoln. She had never been to Omaha, a little over fifty miles away.

Still, Caril was in Charlie's view the only good thing that had ever happened to him. Before they met, his adult life loomed ahead of him, threatening to be as bleak and hopeless as his childhood. He had few abilities or social skills which could gain him respect, except among those people who were as backward as he was. He could only work at menial jobs and had trouble keeping those. Some people considered him retarded and others avoided him because of his temper. He did have potential as an artist but lacked the diligence to develop the talent. He hid behind his movie-star image, but he could never conceal his size, his bowed legs, his speech impediment, his mind.

Caril didn't care about any of those things. She probably never recognized Charlie's weaknesses. She was impressed by his cars, his toughness, his looks, and — despite his poverty — the way he could give her almost anything she wanted. Asked about various possessions in her room — jewelry, a radio, a phonograph — Charlie said, "If it's there I got it for her."

He talked at length to Reinhardt about his feelings toward Caril, and the criminologist used the material in his book. Charlie said that Caril meant more to him than anything had before. Without her he would be thrust back into the world he hated so much. He felt that they had to be separated from everyone else. Caril almost even made him stop hating himself. He saw himself as reflected in her eyes and he looked good. She liked whatever he did, even liked the fact he lived in a dump — probably because she lived in one too. She liked his bowed legs, said that the more bowed they were, the better she liked them. She liked his size — they made a good match — and she liked running her fingers through his red hair. Once she pulled out a hair and looked at it and said she loved every hair in his head. But Charlie said that loving Caril didn't make him able to love anyone else. He had heard somewhere that when a person loves someone he loves everyone a little more, but this wasn't true with him. It gave him a thrill to tell the world to go to hell. He couldn't see how he could want to live at all, even with Caril, if he didn't have his hatred to sustain him.

He and Caril fought at times, but they never argued about how much they cared for each other, and he said they never held anything back from each other. There would be times when they would lie together and look at the same star, or run their hands over each other's faces, and they would realize that the world had given them to each other. And Charlie intended to make the world leave them alone.

Since his early teen-age years, Charlie had hauled garbage part-time on the Neiderhaus garbage route with his older brother Rodney; then when he dropped out of school at sixteen he got a full-time job at the Western Newspaper Union warehouse. His main duties were to unload trucks and bale paper. He never advanced and seldom was given a raise. The company manager, John Hedge, who judged Charlie retarded, said in court, "Sometimes you'd have to tell him something two or three times. Of all the employees in the warehouse, he was the dumbest man we had." He often fell asleep on the job, and one day he set up a sun lamp and went to sleep under it, getting a bad burn. He was usually building a hot rod on the side, charging parts to the company, then having the purchases taken out of his pay. The parts frequently came to more than Charlie made, and Hedge finally had to put a stop to it.

While Charlie was baling paper one day, the handle on the baling machine slipped out of his hand and struck him in the corner of the left eye. It knocked him out briefly, and he was taken to the Lincoln Clinic where he required several stitches. He had headaches and depressions after that, several times a week, for the rest of his short life. He ate aspirin constantly but said it didn't do much good.

While working at the paper company, he and Caril had had an arrangement to get her home from school. He had taught her almost a year before how to drive. The paper company was near Whittier Junior High, which she attended, so in the mornings Charlie would park the car near the school and leave the keys under the floor mat. Caril would drive the car home, and he would catch a ride to her house later with friends from the paper company. The arrangement worked for a while, but one afternoon Caril didn't look when she pulled out of the parking place and hit a passing car, which knocked Charlie's Ford back into a parked car. No one was hurt but all the cars were damaged. Caril got off lighter than Charlie, even though he wasn't there. She had to write a 500-word essay at the police department about driving without a license. Charlie got a ticket for letting her drive his car and had to leave home over the incident.

Guy Starkweather had gotten a $150 loan to help Charlie buy the car, and the title was in both of their names. He demanded Charlie swear he would never let Caril drive it again, but Charlie refused. In an unusual gesture of defiance — he rarely would stand up to his father — Charlie had her drive it in sight of his younger brothers. Enraged, Guy attacked Charlie in the living room of their small frame house, knocking him into a window. Guy Starkweather's account in court of the incident was milder than the statements of others who were there: "He more or less wanted to go out on his own, and I had forbid him to let Caril drive his car. He slipped, stumbled, and fell back through the window. Charlie had slapped me, and I slapped one back. The windows are low, and he fell into it."

Guy told him to get out and never come back. Charlie was so mad that when he got into his car, he rammed his fist into

the door window. Bob Von Busch saw it all and took Charlie
over to the rooming house on 10th Street where he and Barbara — by now his wife — lived. Charlie stayed with them for
several weeks — until the landlady said that two young married
people didn't need a third party around and he would have to
move into a room across the hall. He was still living there
when he committed his first murder several months later.

After Charlie's fight with his father, he stayed away from
home a while but finally started stopping by to visit and grab a
quick meal. Still, he never really forgave his father. Caril was
the center of his life now — Bob and Charlie's brother Rodney
had both gotten married; his other older brother, Leonard, had
taken a job in Washington State. Charlie showed his devotion
to Caril by spending everything he made on her. One gift,
which she was wearing when they were captured, was a gold
heart with "Caril" engraved on one side and "Chuck" on the
other. On October 14, 1957, soon after Charlie had been
kicked out of the house, he and Caril opened a joint savings account at the First National Bank of Lincoln.

John Hedge had been on the verge of firing Charlie, but
Charlie quit first. He said the reason was that Hedge would
hire college boys, whom Charlie had to train to operate the
equipment, and soon the new boys would be making more
money than he was. After he quit he still dropped by from time
to time to visit the friends he had there. They remembered that
he usually would have a new story to tell, stories they knew
weren't true. Once he told them that he and Caril had gotten
married. They asked who had signed for them — since they
were underage — and he said no one. They all knew then that
he had made it up to see how they would take it. Another time
he came in grinning and said, "Well, I'm going to be a father.
Caril's pregnant." This was false also, but it was a rumor that
spread and caused Caril considerable trouble at home.

29

Caril was the real reason Charlie quit the paper company. He needed a job where he could get off work by three in the afternoon, in time to pick her up from school. Rodney got him on the Neiderhaus garbage route again — full-time — and he was usually through by then. The hours were better, but the work was even more demeaning than lifting boxes. And after the hauling was over, there were annoying extra duties which sometimes still tied Charlie up past time for Caril to get out of school.

He was making only forty-two dollars a week at the job, not nearly enough to buy Caril what she wanted and support himself too. Charlie was soon several weeks behind in his rent at the rooming house, and his landlady began locking him out until he could come up with the money. On the nights he was homeless, he often wound up at the Crest station where he hung around with the night attendant, Robert McClung.

In court, in response to questions from County Attorney Elmer Scheele, McClung reflected on those evenings with Charlie. He said that Charlie usually talked about cars, about racing them at Capital Beach and plans for rebuilding them, but McClung knew that he didn't have the money to do most of what he talked about. Charlie was so broke he had to bum cold drink and cigarette money from the attendant. McClung said that Charlie talked about the fight he had had with his father and seemed upset about it. He added, "His conversation didn't always make sense . . . he would talk in circles and his intelligence seemed limited. He affected me as a person who needed help . . . given a decent job or a chance." McClung recalled one night when Charlie drove up with a new paint job on his car and insisted that McClung go out and feel the paint. "I didn't want to go out. I was counting money. He was so emphatic that I feel the car that I went out and felt it, just out of my heart I might say."

Attorney Scheele asked, "Would you say he is like a two-dollar bill or a three-dollar bill?"

"A three-dollar bill."

"How many three-dollar bills have you seen, Mr. McClung?"

"None."

"Then he is like nothing?"

"He is like nothing I have ever seen."

Chapter TWO

By December 1, 1957, Russia had two *Sputniks* in orbit while our overrated *Vanguard* with its basketball-sized satellite had collapsed on the launching pad. President Eisenhower's health was failing and some doubted Nixon's ability to lead. The 101st Airborne had landed at Little Rock, Arkansas. In the early, bleak hours of that morning, Charles Starkweather was steeling himself to begin a life of crime. Driving a light blue 1949 Ford, he pulled out onto Cornhusker Highway, less than a mile from Caril Fugate's house where he had been earlier, and cruised past the Crest service station. It was a little after 3:00 A.M. and six below zero; no one else was on the highway.

Robert Colvert, the twenty-one-year-old attendant, was inside the station's garage, apparently by himself. Sometimes the last attendant, Robert McClung, still stopped in late at night for a cup of coffee, and Charlie drove by twice to satisfy himself that Colvert was alone. The brightly lit driveway of the modern station was empty. Red flags strung on wire between the light poles flapped in the bitter wind, and a giant round sign on a tall iron pole glowed CREST. A sweeping red arrow on the sign curved around the word and pointed at 28.9. Near the pumps, a smaller cardboard sign said in handwritten letters: FRUIT CAKE 98¢. A large billboard beside the station read: IN ALL 48 STATES GET THE BEST! ASK FOR ETHYL!

No cars pulled in, or even passed on the highway, and Charlie thought that probably no one would be stopping during the minutes he needed. But he wasn't quite sure enough. He pulled in the station, went in the office for a pack of Winstons, waited around a minute, and left. Shortly he returned, this time buying some gum, and left again. The station could have been on the moon for all the business it was doing.

He drove around again, then pulled to a stop on the side of the highway and tied a bandanna around his head, covering all of his face beneath the eyes. He put on a hunting cap to hide his red hair and slipped on his leather gloves. On the seat beside him was a 12 guage shotgun he had taken the day before from the garage of Bob Von Busch's cousin, Sonny Von Busch. Whether Colvert lived or died depended on if he recognized Charlie through the disguise. And he might. He had seen him the two times tonight, and just the other day Colvert had argued with Charlie, refusing him credit when he tried to buy a stuffed toy dog the station had stocked as a Christmas special. It had made Charlie mad, but other than that one time Colvert had seemed nice enough. Charlie had heard, too, that the boy had a nineteen-year-old pregnant wife at home.

Once again, Charlie pulled into the station and parked near the front pumps. When he went inside this time, he took with him the shotgun and a canvas moneybag he had found on his garbage route.

Colvert, who was wearing white Unionalls — sometimes

33

called a "monkey suit" — looked up from a car he was working on and, without a word, walked with Charlie into the station's office. As Charlie said later to one of his interrogators: "He knew what I was there for." Colvert recently had been discharged from the navy where he had been nicknamed "Little Bob." Since his discharge he had allowed his hair to flourish into a swirling pompadour, which seemed to add slightly to his height, but he was still as short as Charlie and weighed only 130 pounds.

In the office, Charlie held out the money sack and told Colvert to fill it up. Colvert quickly emptied the change from his pockets into the bag. Charlie still felt uneasy about somebody driving up, and he ordered the attendant to turn off the outside lights. Colvert went into a supply room at the rear of the office and flipped a switch. Only two lights went out in the drive. Colvert stood in the supply-room door and told Charlie he didn't know where the other switches were. He was new here and hadn't had occasion to use them.

Charlie accepted that and told Colvert to get the rest of the money. Worried that he might be seen, he stepped out of sight in the supply room and held the gun on Colvert through the door. The attendant took some bills and a metal money changer full of coins out of a counter drawer and put it all in the bag — a total of around $108, though later the station manager would estimate $160. Beneath the counter, set in concrete, was a large steel safe. Charlie tapped the heavy wheel around the combination with his gun and ordered Colvert to open it.

Colvert said he didn't know the combination. The owner hadn't taught it to him yet. He said he would open it if he could — it wasn't his money. Charlie studied the young man's pale face, decided he was telling the truth, and told him to walk out to the car, that they were going for a ride.

Colvert got in on the passenger's side, but Charlie did too, making Colvert slide over under the wheel. Charlie explained later, "I couldn't drive and hold the gun on him at the same time." He had Colvert drive northeast on Cornhusker, then left on 27th Street. They drove down 27th to a lonely, frozen dirt road outside of town called Superior Street.

Superior was one of the roads Lincoln teen-agers drove to when they were riding around or wanted to park. It had a reputation for being spooky and dangerous, partly because it was remote, but mostly because of a dilapidated farmhouse belonging to an old woman the teen-agers called Bloody Mary. Her two-story frame house was located just east of the girdered Salt Creek bridge, and kids challenged each other to pull in her driveway — or even sneak up on her front porch. There was a rumor that Bloody Mary was a witch, but a more tangible danger was involved in the dares. She would fire at any intruder with a shotgun loaded with rock salt. Later, in the sixties, the thrill of cruising Bloody Mary's ended when someone was killed by a shotgun blast in the head. The harassed old woman had stopped using rock salt.

About three quarters of a mile west of Bloody Mary's, near some railroad tracks, Charlie had Colvert stop the car. He told him to get out. Colvert, who was not wearing a coat, at first refused but Charlie jabbed the gun into the young man's ribs and forced him out. He then slid across the seat himself and was getting out on the driver's side when Colvert suddenly turned and grabbed the barrel of the shotgun. Charlie said later, "I got into a helluva fight and shooting gallery. He shot himself the first time. He had ahold of the gun from the front, and I cocked it and we was messing around and he jerked it and the thing went off." The blast knocked Colvert down, but he started to get up again. Charlie quickly put another shell in the gun, held the barrel against the back of Colvert's head, and pulled the trigger. "He didn't get up anymore," Charlie said.

He left the body where it lay in the middle of the road, drove east to the bridge by Bloody Mary's, then remembered that the empty shell from the first shot had been ejected when he reloaded, and he hadn't picked it up. He drove back to the still form in the road, found the empty cartridge in the gravel next to the body, and continued on west to 27th. Passing the Crest station a few minutes later, he noticed a car by the front pumps, waiting for service.

He got on 10th Street, heading for his room, and passed the squat red brick National Guard Armory on the way. A large sign in front said: SLEEP WELL. YOUR NATIONAL GUARD IS AWAKE. But all the windows were dark.

Charlie slept until around nine the next morning. When he got up, he showered and changed clothes, counted the money, then went over to Caril's and told her about it. But he told her another person had done the shooting. "She wasn't fooled," he said later. "She saw right through that. She knew me like a book." He put a box of empty coin wrappers from the robbery in Caril's room, and the two went for a ride around town with the murder weapon still under the seat. By evening, he was getting nervous about keeping the shotgun and threw it into Salt Creek by the South Street bridge, near Neihoff's junkyard. He put the coin changer in the sand of the shallow creek, grinding it under with his foot.

On Monday, Lincoln *Star* banner headlines read LINCOLNITE SLAIN: THEFT MOTIVE SEEN. Cold-blooded murder was rare in Lincoln — this was the third murder for the year of any kind in Lancaster County — and for some time it was the major news event in the area. Everybody in town was talking about it.

In the midst of the excitement, Charlie went to the Clothing Resale and Gift Shop on North 12th and bought about ten dollars' worth of used clothing for himself. He paid for the clothes in change, despite newspapers and radio station reports that a considerable amount of change had been taken. But in other ways he took considerable precautions. The Crest station was having its drive paved, but part of it was still dirt, so he changed the tires on his Ford so the tracks couldn't be traced. He painted the car black, removed the grille, and painted the interior of the grille area red. When his friends asked why he painted the car, he said, "I had to. These guys got drunk the other night and spotted it with a lot of different-colored paint." After a few days, he fished the shotgun out of the river, cleaned it up somewhat, and put it back in Sonny Von Busch's garage. While he was doing this, two deputies and two jail trusties were wading the same creek down by Bloody Mary's, searching with garden rakes for the gun. On December 10, lest his absence from the Crest station arouse suspicion, he and Caril stopped by and inspected one of the stuffed toy poodles on sale for Christmas. One day that month he stopped by to see his buddies at the paper company, and one of them asked jokingly what he was going to do with all that money he got off Colvert. He grinned and said, "Oh, I got lots of things to do with it."

Lincoln law-enforcement agencies drew considerable criticism from the public for not solving the murder. The agencies, principally the sheriff's office and the police department, blamed the public for failing to cooperate.

Since the murder occurred outside the city limits, the sheriff's office, under Sheriff Merle Karnopp, was responsible for solving it. At about five in the morning of the murder, Lincoln police had discovered the Crest station to be open but unattended, and they had radioed in a report. A few minutes later, the operator of the Nebraska Detective Agency, who was making his routine nightly rounds of local business establishments, found a body in white Unionalls on Superior Street.

Sheriff Karnopp ran into difficulties immediately. Two airmen from a nearby air base were riding with the detective who had found the body, and one of them didn't want to get involved. To avoid the airman some unexplained "personal embarrassment," the detective and the other airman made the report without him, and during the subsequent questioning it became clear that they were withholding information about their other companion. They became prime suspects, which slowed down the investigation for several days. Just when that was cleared up, an ex-convict, Philmon Immenschuh, who had recently been arrested on another charge, in Omaha, confessed to the murder. Immenschuh was brought to Lincoln, and it looked as if the case was solved until a polygraph test indicated he hadn't done it. It turned out he was suffering the aftereffects of a drinking binge, didn't think the prison in Omaha was doing enough to help his problem, and he wanted to be put in the Lincoln prison where he hoped to get better treatment.

Also, true to Charlie's comic-book education, the sheriff's office operated partly on the assumption that the murderer was a transient. They conducted spot traffic checks and called motels around town. The Crest station was inspected by the sheriff's office for clues, and the attendants were asked if any suspicious people had been hanging around. Robert McClung mentioned Charlie. He said he had talked to him for hours on end about cars but had never bothered to learn his name. "Sometimes he fell asleep reading comic books," McClung said to reporters later. "He probably slept in his car a dozen times near the station. He had me wake him up at about 4:15 A.M. for his garbage job." McClung also told reporters that the investigators hadn't seemed very interested when he told them about Charlie. Weeks later, someone from the police department, which had now entered the case, came by the station and asked the manager about the redheaded kid. The manager said he didn't know of such a person, but thought McClung might have been talking about Dale Gardner, called "Pinky," whom everyone knew. The lead was dropped.

Mrs. John Kamp, owner of the Clothing Resale and Gift Shop, reported to the police on December 2 that someone had bought $9.55 worth of used wearing apparel, paying the bill with change. She had heard that about ten dollars in change had been taken from the Crest Station: "I told them all about what he looked like, his red hair and a slouch and how short he was, and that I'd recognize him from a photo. The detective took it all down and then he came back later with some pictures, but none of them were the boy." Five days later Mrs. Kamp saw Charlie again as she was waiting for a bus. "I was frightened because I thought he might take a swing at me if the police had questioned him." She didn't call the police again because she assumed they had already talked to him. Charlie had been trading at the store for about a year and a half, but, like the Crest attendant, Mrs. Kamp hadn't learned his name.

Police reports conflict with the storekeeper's account: "The identification actually given by Mrs. Kamp was of a male, unkempt individual, approximately 25 or 30 years of age. She could not give any description of the color of his hair, or the color of his eyes, due to the fact that at the time of his visit he was wearing a hunting hat, and thick eyeglasses."

Much later, after ten more people had been murdered and Charlie had been captured, Harold G. Robinson, a trained investigator of police activities, was brought to Lincoln from California to do an independent study of the handling of the Starkweather case. The investigation, considered by some to be a whitewashing, found nothing inadequate about Lincoln law enforcement. In connection with the Colvert murder, Robinson wrote that in the absence of tangible clues, the bizarre circumstances of the crime — a person known by employees of the sta-

tion holding it up with a shotgun in full view of the highway —
made it impossible to draw conclusions which would have led
to a rapid apprehension.

Now, seventeen years later, Sheriff Merle Karnopp — tall
and trim, distinguished-looking with his thick wavy hair
combed straight back and deep lines etched in his face — sits at
his desk, thumbing through old police photos of the Colvert
murder. He ruminates: "It was bitter cold the night we had to
go out to Superior Street. I'll never forget the way that wind
cut. And, you know, the Colvert boy didn't even have a jacket
on when we found him." He shuffles the pictures into a neat
stack like they were a deck of cards and looks up. "The Colvert
case was a difficult one — one of our hardest. But we would
have solved it if we'd had the time. I'm convinced of that.
Charlie just didn't give us the time."

After killing Colvert, Charlie told Reinhardt, he regained
some of the lost feeling of peace and happiness he remembered
from his childhood. The only times he had come close to
recapturing the feeling before the murder were on hunting trips
when he could be off in the woods alone with nature. But now
he was no longer haunted by memories of his first day in
school. He had, at least temporarily, evened the score and
could see the sun set in its tender glory.

He had money. He had a girl. He had killed and not been
bothered by it. It gave him an enormous feeling of power. He
now operated outside the laws of man. He felt as if he were in-
visible, could do just as he pleased, take what he wanted. The
law was helpless against him. Here he was, right in the middle
of town, and they were running all around him like the stupid
chickens he had fed as a child. At night he slept deeply.

He bought new things for Caril but only secondhand clothes
for himself. Reinhardt wrote that Charlie felt that old clothes
were like wearing another man's skin, but he was happy with

them — they covered him and he didn't have to worry about ruining them. When he bought his clothes, he had paid with the stolen change just to get rid of it. He wasn't worried about the old lady at the store — he traded there often. He was sure she knew him. She wouldn't think anything of it, despite the newspaper and radio urging everyone to report anything that might be of help.

After buying the clothes he had gone back to the old downtown tenement house and put them on. He oiled and combed his hair until it was a work of art and then went downstairs to pay his back rent. It made him feel good to be able to pay it. The old landlady, Mrs. May Hawley, and her husband, Orlin, were glad to see the money. They noticed his clothes and asked how he had suddenly gotten so rich. "I took it out of my savings account," he said.

One day soon after the murder he went over to his folks' house and had breakfast with them. They were back on speaking terms with him, but Charlie knew he would never move back in. He chatted with his mother and father at the breakfast table about the Colvert murder. Charlie was fascinated at how easy it was for him, the killer, to talk about himself as if he were another person. Just before he left he asked them: "I wonder what sort of person it would take to do such a thing?"

Charlie and Caril enjoyed themselves during the weeks after the holdup. They went to all the movies with shooting in them, and they had a wide selection, even in a city as small as Lincoln. Showing at the State Theater was *The Parson and the Outlaw* ("The Day they called the Kid a Coward") — twin-billed with *Escape From San Quentin*. At the Stuart was *Man in the Shadow* ("The kind of hard-fisted entertainment you like so well!"). *Last of the Badmen* was at the Nebraska Theater, and *Pickup Alley* and *The Domino Kid* were showing at the drive-ins. Even though it was winter, the new in-car heaters allowed the drive-ins to stay open. The ads read: NOW! HEATERS THAT REALLY HEAT! ALL NEW IN-CAR HEATERS! HEALTHFUL RADIANT HEAT! OPEN EVERY NITE! ALL WINTER!

Other evenings they stayed alone together in Charlie's room at the tenement house to enjoy the fresh stacks of comics he brought home. Tenement houses were unusual in Nebraska and this one, a two-story gray stone building with over forty separate units, was almost one of a kind in Lincoln. Besides Bob and Barbara Von Busch, a few other members of Caril's family also lived there, including her grandmother, Pansy Street. Caril herself had lived there with her mother, Velda, until Velda married Marion Bartlett and they moved with him to the house on Belmont Avenue. (Velda previously had been married to William Fugate, whom she divorced in 1951. Fugate, over the years, had acquired a police record ranging from contributing to the delinquency of a minor and voyeurism to intoxication and assault.)

Despite her grandmother's protests, Caril spent long hours with Charlie in his room, practicing knife-throwing with him, playing 45s on the record player, eating sweets and other snacks she couldn't get at home. She watched while Charlie practiced drawing a gun, Old West style, on himself in the mirror on the door. He told Reinhardt, "If somebody died everytime I drew that gun, I would've got over a thousand." He drew pictures for her, and she couldn't get over how good he was. (A lot of people couldn't. His father once said proudly to reporters, "Why, he could draw a picture of you and you couldn't tell the difference!")

As far as Charlie was concerned, killing Colvert had cemented his relationship with Caril. It was the first step down a final road they would soon take together. Reinhardt pieced together comments about this from their conversations, and quoted Charlie as saying that time seemed to drag on endlessly after they had made their plans. He knew that they would have some good moments together, and then their race with life would be over — with them together. He believed, when he was with her, that nothing would make him happier than he was at that moment. He still hated people, but he found they didn't bother him like they used to. It used to be that his family was all he had, but now they were only getting in his way. Caril wanted more, he said, after he had killed Colvert, and he knew how to get it for her. He knew how to kill a person now, knew for sure that it didn't bother him. He didn't know why he was like he was, why he could do such things, and he didn't really care. Now he had something worth killing for. For years he had pictured himself dying, but now he had something to live for before he died. Everything was his until the clock ran down.

Fifty days passed between the time Charlie killed Colvert and the time he and Caril began their eight-day murder spree. Charlie admitted to no criminal acts during the fifty days, but on January 4, 1958, a slight acquaintance of Charlie's, seventeen-year-old Jimmy Law, died enroute to the hospital after being shot with a .22 given to him for Christmas. It happened in the evening, while his parents were at a movie. Though there was no note and Jimmy had not seemed despondent, the death was ruled a suicide. Later it was declared an accident. Charlie was not being sought for anything at the time, and the case was not reopened after his capture, but some people in Lincoln still wonder about the coincidence.

The elation Charlie felt from killing Colvert soon ended and he found things closing in on him again. He had become lazy now that he knew how to make fast money, and his brother Rodney had to fire him from the garbage route. Now that he and Caril were closer, their families seemed even more determined to break them up. Guy Starkweather blamed Caril for the fact that Charlie had lost two jobs, thinking that she must be taking away his concentration and ambition. He thought she was using Charlie. Guy said in court, "Charlie seemed to be more changed after he met Miss Fugate. He never caused me any real trouble, exactly, but he was a little bit stubborn. You couldn't reason with him. He would come to it, but not like he had before. He would tell me he was getting tired of me telling him what to do." Caril's parents got to where they couldn't stand the sight of Charlie. They said he was too old for her and would never amount to anything. He couldn't even hold down a job. They began to insult him and argue with him whenever he came over, telling him they had another boy in mind for Caril. And some authorities, including Sheriff Karnopp, suspect that Caril's parents knew he had killed Colvert, or at least knew he had participated in the holdup, and that they were holding it over his head to make him break up with Caril. But this theory is based on the box of empty coin wrappers found in the house, and of course it is possible that the box could have been there without their knowing about it.

The money from the robbery was soon gone. He was behind on the rent and came home one day to find his door padlocked again. He was locked out a whole week in freezing weather and was forced to sleep in an unheated garage he had rented to work on a hot rod. During this week he came down with a bad cold that would torment him until after his capture.

Charlie had reached the breaking point but he didn't recognize it; he saw it as a turning point. He had always known he would die young, but now he had something to live for first. He could be with Caril, they could do what they wanted, and he could leave his mark on the world. He thought of himself as the lowest thing on earth but had convinced himself that others had made him what he was. Later he would say that the world, not Charlie Starkweather, was to blame for the death of eleven people. Reinhardt quoted him as saying: "If you pull the chain on a toilet, you can't blame it for flushing, can you?"

Chapter THREE

ON TUESDAY MORNING, January 21, 1958, Charlie agreed to help his brother for a few hours on the garbage route, and afterward returned to his room to see if the padlock was still on the door. It was. He saw Barbara Von Busch in the hall, started to say something, then turned and left. He was not on good terms with any of Caril's relatives. Caril had started gaining weight, "getting a little thick around the middle," as Sonny Von Busch put it, and the family was sure she was pregnant. Charlie said he had had a confrontation with the Bartletts the previous Sunday about her weight gain.

He had gone to his room on Tuesday to try to get his gun. Perhaps even then he had murder on his mind, though he denied it. Afterward, he went to Rodney's and borrowed a .22 rifle, saying he wanted it to go hunting with Caril's father, Marion Bartlett. This would have been unusual for Marion because he disliked Charlie so much and because he almost never went hunting. Still, Charlie maintained later that they had talked about it a week before and Marion had agreed to go. It could be true. The plans could have been made before Charlie's relationship with the family got quite so bad, and he might have pursued the arrangement in an effort to get back on good terms with them. Marion worked as a night watchman at the Watson Brothers Transportation Company and at least would have had the time for an afternoon in the woods before going on duty.

In 1958 much of the Belmont area was a slum. Belmont Avenue — at least the block where the Bartletts lived — had a particularly squalid look about it, and the Bartletts' house was a tiny five-room shack, covered with imitation-brick asphalt siding, and only recently had acquired an indoor bathroom. The house was in a constant state of disorder and disrepair because of various home improvements Marion Bartlett had started but never finished. The yard was a frozen mire littered with trash, building materials, and automobile parts. A double row of long boards, serving as a sidewalk, stretched along the driveway to the front door. Around back was an outhouse and a chicken coop, and near the kitchen door of the house was a wooden clothesline pole with a mop dangling from it, the mop-head frozen over the crossbar. A medium-sized black watchdog named Nig was attached by a long chain to the base of the pole.

When Charlie pulled his Ford to a stop out on the street by the Bartletts' mailbox, Nig gave one obligatory bark and dragged his chain to the front of the house to greet him. The exact sequence of events that followed is blurred because of conflicting testimony. The conflict centered around what part, if any, Caril played in what happened.

In one of Charlie's later confessions, made to Chief Deputy Dale Fahrnbruch, he gave the most detailed version of what happened. The following account is based on that confession, but it should be understood that there is no way of telling if Charlie's statements are absolutely true.

He said he went to the Bartletts' at around 1 P.M. with the .22 and two small multicolored rugs for Mrs. Bartlett. According to Charlie, the rugs were carpet samples which he had found mounted on discarded display boards in a junkyard. Mrs. Bartlett had indicated earlier that she wouldn't mind having them. He walked across the boards in the yard with the rifle, the rugs, and two boxes of shells in the pockets of his motorcycle jacket. The shells were to be used on the jackrabbits he and Marion had agreed to go hunting for. Nig's bark caused Mrs. Bartlett, a slight woman no bigger than Caril, to open the kitchen door as Charlie came up on the back porch.

She asked if those were the rugs and he said they were. Charlie took the rugs into the living room, a small, cluttered area with a piano, an old couch, a portable clothes closet, a TV, and a few chairs. Four or five long pieces of rope used as clothesline were stretched from wall to wall on nails. He sat down on the couch, untied the strings from around the rolled-up rugs, and spread them around on the bare Congoleum floor.

After a moment, Mrs. Bartlett came in, looked at the rugs, and left the room without speaking. Marion was in the kitchen with Caril's two-and-a-half-year-old half sister, Betty Jean, who was crying. Charlie sat in the living room for ten or fifteen minutes, uncertain what to do. The couple seemed in a bad mood, and he had never liked being around Betty Jean. According to Charlie, Caril didn't like her either. He said later to Fahrnbruch, "Betty Jean was a little snot, that was my opinion. Caril's opinion was that she was a monster. She called her about every name you could think of. She had a lot of reasons. You couldn't make her mind, and she was always getting somebody in trouble. She got me in trouble a few times. She'd go flying in to her old man or mom and say I hit her. One reason

Caril didn't like her was she was a step-sister. Marion treated Betty Jean far more than he ever did Caril. Caril used to gripe about it all the time."

Charlie dusted his gun while he sat on the couch, inserted the bolt action, then went back through the house to see what had happened to everybody. Mr. Bartlett was lying down in the southwest bedroom, and Velda and Betty Jean were on the bed in Caril's bedroom. Betty Jean was playing with the radio on a stand by the bed. Charlie remarked later that the radio, like most of what Caril owned, was a present from him. He had thought Marion had given him a dirty look when he first came in the house, and now he was afraid to ask him if they were still going hunting. He asked Mrs. Bartlett instead.

According to Charlie, she said, "I don't think so."

"Why not?"

"He's just not going to go."

Charlie propped the gun against the wall and sat down on a wooden crate to talk things over. Velda sat up on the bed, annoyed. "Chuck, you're going to have to leave, and I don't want you ever to come back."

"Why?"

"I don't want you to see Caril no more."

They were soon in a loud argument, and Charlie yelled at Mrs. Bartlett, "You go to hell!"

Later he said, "She didn't say nothing. She just got up and slammed the shit out of me . . . in the face." He couldn't remember which hand she used because, "It came at me too fast."

Charlie said that she hit him two or three times, and he ran out of the house, forgetting the rifle. He drove around the block, then returned to pick up the gun and "to find out what the hell was the matter."

Again, he went through the back porch to the kitchen door,

the most commonly used entrance to the house, and knocked. Mrs. Bartlett opened the door without speaking and he went inside. Marion, who was of medium build but powerful from years of manual labor, was waiting in the kitchen. Charlie said later, "The old man started chewing me out. I said to hell with him and was going to walk out through the front door, and he helped me out. Kicked me right in the ass. My tail hurt for three days."

Hutson's Grocery was the main place to shop in the area, and the closest store to the Bartletts'. When Charlie was kicked out, he drove there to use the phone. Since the Bartletts didn't have a phone, Charlie and Caril frequently used the one at Hutson's. Sometimes they would take advantage of the free business phone, but this time Charlie used the pay phone. He was asked later if he had done that so people in the store couldn't hear the conversation. He hadn't. "I just had a dime and I thought I'd use it." The call he made was to Watson Brothers Transportation Company, where Marion Bartlett worked. He told the woman who answered that Mr. Bartlett was ill and wouldn't be in for a few days.

Charlie returned to the Bartletts' but they wouldn't let him in, so he hung around outside, playing with Nig for about half an hour, waiting for the time to pick Caril up from school. Around three he got in the car to go after her but discovered he was having transmission trouble. Instead of trying to make it to Whittier Junior High, he took the car to the house of some relatives, the Griggses, a block away, and parked it. Then he waited on the Bartletts' back porch for Caril to walk home.

Nig soon started barking from around the side of the house, and Charlie heard the high-pitched voices of Caril and Velda. He let himself in the kitchen door and found them in Caril's bedroom. "They was yelling their heads off," Charlie told Fahrnbruch. "He was! He wasn't! He was! He wasn't!" Finally, Caril went into the bathroom, leaving Charlie to face Velda. Betty Jean was jumping up and down on the bed in a frenzy.

Charlie said that Velda yelled that he had made Caril pregnant. Then "She got up and slapped the shit out of me again . . . in the head . . . both sides. I hauled off and hit her one back . . . in the head . . . my hand wasn't closed . . . it knocked her back a couple of steps. She let out a cry, a war cry or something, and the old man came flying in. He picked me up . . . by the neck . . . and started carrying me to the front door. I kicked him somewhere and he put me down. We started wrestling around in the front room." Asked if he was ever on the floor during the fight, he said, "I might have got down there a few times. I don't ever think he did. Then he took off for the other room. I knew what he was heading for, so I thought I'd head for the same thing."

Charlie ran in Caril's bedroom and had just loaded the single-shot .22 when Marion came in with a claw hammer raised over his head. "I just wheeled around and fired." Marion, hit in the head by the bullet, collapsed in front of Caril's dresser. According to Charlie, Caril walked in, stared at her stepfather, then they left him, going into the living room.

In the meantime, Velda had run into the kitchen and now returned with a foot-long black-handled kitchen knife. Charlie said later, "The old lady Bartlett said she was going to chop my head off, and I loaded the gun again . . . the old lady started to take a few steps towards me . . . And Caril jerked the gun away and said she'd blow her to hell . . . The old lady got mad and knocked her down . . . I grabbed the gun from Caril . . . I just turned around and shot her." She was hit in the side of the face.

Asked by Fahrnbruch if she fell down, he said, "Well, not quite . . . she went on by, heading for the little girl . . . she just stopped, and I thought she was going to pick up the girl, but she never, she just turned around and looked at me again . . . and I hit her with the butt of the gun . . . she fell down, but she wasn't quite all the way down, so I hit her again . . . she just laid there . . . after I hit the old lady, I just came up with the butt of the gun and hit the little girl . . . she fell down against the kind of table . . . stood there screaming . . . Caril was yelling at her to shut up."

Then Charlie said Caril told him her stepfather was moving around in the bedroom. "I picked up the knife that the old lady had . . . and started to walk in there, in the bedroom . . . and the little girl kept yelling, and I told her to shut up, and I started to walk again, and just turned around and threw the kitchen knife I had at her . . . they said it hit her in the throat, but I thought it hit her in the chest . . . I went on into the bedroom. Mr. Bartlett was moving around quite a bit, so I tried to stab him in the throat, but the knife wouldn't go in, and I just hit the top part of it with my hand, and it went in."

Because there were no surviving witnesses to the murders, all that investigators had to go on later were Charlie's and Caril's testimonies and external evidence. For most of his life, Charlie had a reputation for lying. Nothing he said was taken very seriously. He was fond of telling people he was from Texas, perhaps to justify his broad-rimmed cowboy hat and blue and white cowboy boots, or maybe he just thought people would think of him differently if they believed he was from the Lone Star State. He once told Bob Von Busch and Rodney that he had a chrome-plated engine in his hot rod when there was no engine in it at all.

His account of the eight-day murder spree changed frequently, depending on his mood and to whom he was talking. He made at least seven different confessions in the form of lengthy statements, letters, and notes. One was written on the wall of his jail cell. In his early statements he said that Caril had nothing to do with any of the murders — she was his hostage. Then he said that those statements were "hogwash" and had been made to protect her; she actually had been a willing accomplice. Even though he was a known liar and killer, the more Charlie talked, the more it seemed possible to some authorities that Caril could have killed some of the victims herself. But having now spent over half of her life in prison, Caril still maintains that she was an unwilling hostage.

She says that she wasn't even dating Charlie when the murders occurred — she had broken up with him the previous Sunday (the day Charlie said her parents accused him of making Caril pregnant). In court, in response to a question by her lawyer, John McArthur, Caril said: "He came down and he came in the house, and we were doing the washing, and he started spouting off about different things and accusing me of going out with other boys, saying nasty things, and I told him to leave and not to come back and I didn't want to ever see him again. And my mother was out in the kitchen and so was my little sister. I went out in the kitchen and I told my mother that I told him to go away, and she told him to go away. And his face turned red, and he got mad about it, and he was hitting his hand with his fist.

"And he asked me if I never wanted to see him again, and I said, yes, I never wanted to see him again. And he says, 'all right,' and hung around for a few minutes, and he went out the door and slammed it."

"Caril," her lawyer asked, "up before that time what did Charlie mainly talk about?"

"He talked mainly about, he was a big sheriff and all that, he was always telling stories . . . he'd say, oh, just tell little stories about being sheriff and how many Indians he caught and everything."

Charlie's first formal statement, given to County Attorney Elmer Scheele, said that Caril was still at school when he had gone up to the Bartletts' kitchen door and was let in. Before she came home, he said, he murdered the family. He then hid the bodies and told Caril her family was being held hostage at an old couple's house where he rented the garage for his hot rod. The old couple, the Southworths, were going to rob a bank, and if anything went wrong her parents would be killed. With this story he supposedly was able to keep her in the house for six days and then was able to make her stay with him all the way to Wyoming where they were captured.

This, basically, was Caril's story, too. Her lawyer, John McArthur, said: "This girl was introduced into this horrible sequence of events by opening the door and having a gun stuck in her face. Hers was really a story of a child in fear of her life for eight terrifying days, a child who believed that not only her own life was in danger but also the lives of her family. She did not know they were dead. If people knew the truth, they would realize that Caril Fugate was no criminal. She was Starkweather's victim, as were all the other victims of Starkweather's madness. Must we condemn Caril for failing to do what no one in Nebraska could do: Stop Starkweather? She was no accomplice. She was a captive."

Caril, interrogated by Chief Deputy Dale Fahrnbruch, said, "He told me my folks were over to that old lady's house where he'd seen the hot rod, I guess that's what you call it. He said if I done what he said they wouldn't be hurt . . . Well, I didn't believe him at first. I kept saying, 'I don't believe you.' "

"And then what happened?" Fahrnbruch asked.

"And then I went out in the kitchen, and I either plugged in the coffee, or he did."

One of Charlie's later stories said that Caril "finished off" her mother with a knife and clubbed to death her baby sister. And another confession was in the form of a letter which was found

53

in Charlie's jacket pocket when he was captured. The letter gave the impression of having been written by both of them — it was from both of their points of view — but Charlie admitted he had done the actual writing. It was addressed "for the law only":

"This is for the cops or law-men who fines us. Caril and i are writing this so that you and ever body will know what has happem. On tue. day 7 days befor you have seen the bodys of ny non, dad and baby sister, there dead because of ne and chuck, chuck cane down that tue. day happy and full of joke's but when he cane in nom said for hin to get out and never come back, chuck look at her, "and said *why*." at that ny dad got nad and be gin to hit hin and was pushing hin all over the room, then chuck got nad and there was no stoping hin, he had his gun whit hin cause hin and my dad was going hunting, well chuck pull it and the [drawing of a bullet] cane out and ny dad drop to the foor, at this ny non was so nad the she had a [drawing of a knife] and was going to cut hin she Knot the gun from chucks hands, chuck just stood there saying he was sorry he didn't want to do it. i got chucks gun and stop my non fron killing chuck. betty Jean was yelling so loud i hit her with the gun about 10 tines she would not stop chuck had the [drawing of a knife] so he was about 10 steps fron her, he let it go it stop some when by her head. ne and chuck just look at then for about 4 hrs . . ."

According to Charlie's detailed statement to Fahrnbruch, after he had stabbed his bone-handled hunting knife, which was similar in shape to a bowie knife, into Marion Bartlett's throat several times, he still wasn't sure if it was enough to kill him. "I didn't want to go in the other room and then have him walk in there again." He sat on the edge of the bed and watched Mr. Bartlett for about five minutes, until it was clear the dying man wasn't going to get up, then he went in the kitchen for a glass of water. He said later, "Caril came in the kitchen and asked what we were going to do with them. I said, 'What do you think we ought to do?'"

According to Charlie, Caril, without answering, went back in the living room and sat on the couch. Charlie followed her in and asked, "What's the matter?"

"Nothing."

"We sure got ourselves in a helluva mess."

"Well, it's what we always wanted."

Charlie claimed that he and Caril had often talked about running away, about leaving town if they ever had to "bump off" her parents. If this is true, their motives are vague. The talk could have grown out of resentment because the Bartletts were trying to break them up, but another possibility is Sheriff Karnopp's theory that the Bartletts were threatening to turn in Charlie in connection with the Colvert murder.

"We better get them cleaned up," Caril said, according to Charlie.

"Don't worry about it. I'll do it myself." He reloaded his gun in case somebody came in, and he turned on the television. "I don't even remember what was on," he told Fahrnbruch. "I just wanted some noise. It was too quiet."

They sat staring at the TV for a while. Then Charlie got up to face the grisly task of disposing of the bodies. Deciding first to wrap them up like mummies, he cut down most of the clothesline hanging around the house and gathered rugs, rags, bedclothes, and building paper. He tied rope around Mrs. Bartlett's knees, then wrapped her up in a quilt and a green fiber rug. Betty Jean was still bleeding so much he put her in the kitchen sink while he wrapped her in a quilt. He emptied some of the garbage out of a cardboard box in the kitchen and replaced it with the baby's body. He put the box on the back porch, dragged Mrs. Bartlett's body out with it, then took the box across the backyard to the outhouse. Shortly, he returned to the outhouse with the body of Mrs. Bartlett and stuffed it down the toilet opening. He placed the box with the baby's body on the toilet seat.

There was a considerable amount of blood on the floors in the house, and he wiped some of it up with rags, putting off the difficult task of disposing of the large, heavy body of Mr. Bartlett. Finally, though, he dragged the body into the kitchen, wrapped it in a blue sheet, and tied it with clothesline around the ankles, knees, chest, and head. He tied one of Caril's scarfs around the head and, over the scarf, wrapped an army blanket. Then he rolled the whole body up in heavy green building paper he found in Mr. Bartlett's tool room at the back of the house.

When he tried to take the awkward bundle outside, he found it wouldn't go through the back door. He had to remove the screen with a screwdriver to make room. Then he half carried, half dragged the body out to the chicken coop and put it inside on the ground next to the north wall. He left, then returned with the screen door and placed it over the bundle.

Police later thought that the door had been used as a litter to carry the body. Because there were no drag marks on the ground from the house to the chicken coop, they assumed somebody — probably Caril — had helped Charlie carry it out. Charlie, however, denied using the door for that purpose.

Though removing the bodies from the house and hiding them was obviously necessary, the place and method Charlie chose caused speculation on the part of psychologists involved in his trial. Wouldn't a person capable of planning have buried the bodies? Why would he put them so close to where he would be staying the next six days? Dr. John Steinman, testifying for the defense, said he thought it was an indication of a diseased mind. Noting similarities in the way the Bartletts and later victims were disposed of, he said: "Putting them in these types of places is a sort of fantasy children sometimes have — throw them in the toilet, flush them down. And I think all through this there is a desire to be caught and punished."

Caril was in the rocking chair in the living room when he came back in the house, Charlie told Fahrnbruch, but he noticed more rags on the floor than when he had left. And Marion's set of false teeth was beside the box of rags Charlie had been using. The teeth hadn't been there before, and he decided Caril had started doing some of the cleaning but had given up. He finished the job, straightened up the house in general, and sprinkled some perfume around to cover the lingering smell of blood. He put one of the new rugs in Caril's room to replace the one now wrapped around the body of Mrs. Bartlett. Under the bed in the Bartletts' bedroom, he found a box of .410 shells and loaded a shotgun that belonged to Mr. Bartlett. He found a .32 pistol that Mrs. Bartlett kept in the kitchen, but it was empty and he could find no shells for it.

Toward evening, he walked down to Hutson's Grocery and bought three bottles of Pepsi-Cola, the soft drink they both preferred, and a large bag of potato chips. Finally, Caril fell asleep on the couch and Charlie dozed off in the rocker. Sometime during the night he woke up to a humming sound and saw a test pattern on the TV set. The center of the pattern was made up of circles within circles, and lines like moon rays emanated from them. The pattern looked like a bright, glaring eye, with the rays seeming to reach out until they filled the whole room with a ghostly light. Charlie turned the set off and lay down on the couch beside Caril, wrapping himself around her. She awoke, protesting, but he clung to her and after a moment she relaxed. Soon they were both asleep again.

The fact that they lived in the house together for almost a

57

week is one of the more bizarre aspects of the Starkweather-Fugate case. It would take, it seems, something less than human, a monster, to be able to stay so long at the scene of a multiple murder, with the putrefying corpses only feet away in the back yard. And if one believes Caril knew about the murders, or was involved, the act almost defies explanation except in terms of pathology.

Later, after their capture, Charlie was studied rather extensively by psychologists, and his mental aberrations were defined. But Caril's defense, unlike Charlie's, was not insanity, so little was done with her in that regard. Even today, Caril remains to many an enigma. In all her years in prison, she has done nothing to indicate a severe mental disorder, yet there have been patterns of moodiness, personality changes, emotional outbursts, and an overall slowness in maturing. Some people find it difficult to believe she had an active part in the murders because, despite any personality quirks, she has always seemed relatively normal. It is unfortunate that an extensive psychological study was not done on Caril. The fact that she had a sexual deviate and alcoholic father, William Fugate, certainly poses questions which need answering.

Intense interrogation of both Charlie and Caril revealed most of what took place during the six days in the Bartlett house. Their stories were almost identical, the only significant difference being that Caril claimed she knew nothing about the death of her family. She maintained that everything she did during the six days was done under the assumption that her family was being held hostage. She claimed that she cooperated with Charlie out of fear for the family's safety.

About six-thirty in the morning of the second day, Charlie and Caril were awakened by a knock on the door. It was one of Caril's schoolmates, a girl named Bonnie, who usually walked with Caril to school. Caril told her she was sick and wasn't going today. Shortly after that, the milkman came. Charlie hid in the bedroom with a gun while Caril bought two bottles of milk, saying she would pay later. When the bread man came, Caril took two loaves of bread on credit.

For breakfast they had bacon, eggs, and toast. To Charlie the best week in his life was under way. Reinhardt quoted him as saying that they lived like kings, that he had never had a more wonderful time, that at last there was nobody to order them around. He felt no guilt because of what he had done. It had been necessary, done in self-defense, and now that it was done the course of his life was clear. He had to elude capture for as long as possible, using whatever means necessary, and derive whatever pleasures he could in the time left to him.

Later on the second day, Charlie went to Hutson's again and bought more Pepsis and potato chips, and also chewing gum, ice cream, candy, and sunflower seeds — all things Caril's step-father wouldn't let her have because he thought they cost too much. Probably, though, they bought these items with his money.

Caril claimed that Charlie tied her up when he left the house, but he denied it. He said he did tie her up once but only as a ruse. "We started talking about what the hell we'd do if we ever got caught . . . we was trying to make up a story, and it didn't work too well . . . I thought if we got caught we'd make up like she was hostage, you know, and we'd start messing around and make it look like it . . . took rope and put it around the hands and feet, and untied it . . . made it look like she was tied up."

Asked by Fahrnbruch how many times he had sexual relations with Caril while at the home, Charlie said, "Every night and morning, and twice on Sunday . . . it might have been five or six times on Sunday, I don't know. Nobody came out Sunday." Charlie had found that his sexual appetite had increased and he fed it continuously. "We was making love all the time. But everytime I'd get going the goddam dog would start barking his head off."

Chief Deputy Dale Fahrnbruch, the principal interrogator on the case besides Scheele, got a 166-page statement from Caril which, because of legal advice, she never signed. However, she did attest to its accuracy, as reported in a Lincoln *Star* article, published on February 6, 1958. Fahrnbruch learned from this statement that Caril's sexual relationship with Charlie was, in part, sodomic. Fahrnbruch asked her many questions about this; on the surface the questions may seem cruel and degrading, but he later explained he was trying to find the extent of Charlie's regard for her. Did he treat her like a helpless hostage? Or did he treat her in a way that indicated concern and affection? It was important for the prosecution's case that they find out if Caril *behaved* like a prisoner.

Fahrnbruch asked Caril, "Do you know what a penis is?"

"Yes."

"Did he at any time have his penis out of his trousers?"

"Yes."

"And what was the reason for that?"

"Well, I don't know what you mean."

"All right, did he at any time put his penis up to your sexual organs?"

"Yes."

"And did he stick it in very far?"

"No."

"Did he put it in slightly?"

"He didn't put it in an inch."

"He put it in less than an inch?"

"Yes."

"And what did he say?"

"Then he stopped."

60

"Now then, Caril, you told me previously that he also put his penis in your rear end, is that right?"

"Yes."

"And were you undressed at that time?"

"Well, not all the way . . . I still had my nightgown on."

"What sort of nightgown was that?"

"One of them shorties."

"Now, Caril, when he put his penis in your rear end did it hurt more or less than when he put his penis in your sexual organs?"

"It hurt less."

"Now, Caril, when you took off your clothes when you had these sexual intercourses, did you take them off?"

"Not all the time."

"Did he take them off some of the time?"

"Yes."

"Had he kissed you before that happened?"

"I think so."

"In other words, you had been kissing him and he was kissing you?"

"Yes."

When Fahrnbruch first started to question Caril about the six days in the house, he was called from the room for a few minutes. While he was gone, there was a brief conversation between Caril and Mrs. Merle Karnopp, the sheriff's wife. Mrs. Karnopp had traveled with Caril part of the way back from Wyoming after the capture, and Caril had talked to her more openly than she now apparently wanted to talk to Fahrnbruch.

Caril now said to Mrs. Karnopp, "I don't remember what went on in the house."

"What do you mean, Caril?"

"I don't remember it at all."

"You don't remember it at all?"

"I don't remember it at all."

"What do you mean, you don't remember it at all?"

"I don't remember what went on."

"Can you remember what you told me, when you talked to me?"

"I don't remember."

Then Fahrnbruch returned, resumed questioning, and Caril gradually regained her memory. According to both her and Charlie, they lived as man and wife for the six days and, with some strange exceptions, they painted a tranquil picture of domestic life. Caril had two parakeets which she continued to feed and water, and they had two dogs to take care of — Nig and a new collie puppy, Kim, which Charlie had bought for Caril at Pet Paradise for five dollars. They played gin rummy a lot, and Charlie later remarked, "I don't know if I was any good or not but I could sure beat her." The television was on constantly. Caril recalled watching *The Thin Man* and, their second night in the house, a Bud Abbott and Lou Costello movie. She went out to the mailbox every afternoon. One day she ran back in with a comic book she had sent off for and spent the rest of the afternoon cutting paper dolls out of a book.

But they were also practicing knife-throwing at the walls, planning their getaway, and Charlie sawed off part of the barrel of Mr. Bartlett's shotgun so the shells would "spread more" when it came time to use it. Whenever someone came to the door, Charlie hid with a gun in the bathroom, or in one of the bedrooms, while Caril turned the visitors away.

By the end of the second day, people were coming by more frequently. A neighbor lady came by for her eggs, which the Bartletts were in the habit of buying for her when they bought their own, and Caril told her they hadn't had a chance to pick them up yet that week. Marion Bartlett's boss and another man stopped by, but Nig kept them away from the house. Caril yelled to them that her father was still sick. The Bartletts were in the process of buying the house, and one evening their landlady came by to discuss the sale but was told the Bartletts weren't home. Caril's schoolmate Bonnie persisted in waking them up every morning, and finally Caril stopped answering when the girl knocked.

Toward the end of the week, the Bartletts' relatives began to wonder if something might be wrong. It wasn't like Velda to stay out of touch so long. Caril's older sister, Barbara, was particularly bothered. Velda had promised her she would bring by some pictures she was having developed of Barbara's new baby. On Saturday, Bob and Barbara wrapped up the baby and took a cab to Belmont Avenue to see what was going on. Also, it was an opportunity to take the baby over to his grandparents' house. He had been sick almost since he had been born and hadn't been there before.

In court they told how they got out of the cab and were hurrying up the wooden sidewalk through misting rain when Caril yelled at them from the front door: "Stop! Don't come any closer!" The Von Busches, shocked and confused, stopped in their tracks, then Bob took the baby from Barbara and ran back to the cab to get him out of the rain. Barbara started to walk on up to the house but Caril yelled for her to stop, so she backed up to where she had been before. The sisters yelled at each other over a distance of about fifteen feet. Caril said that Marion, Velda, and Betty Jean all had the five-day flu and that nobody could come in the house. Doctor's orders. She said that Velda was certain the baby would catch it. Barbara persisted, saying that she would come in by herself, and Caril suddenly opened the screen door and screamed, "Go away! If you know what's best you'll go away so Mother don't get hurt!" Frightened, Barbara returned to the cab.

They were about to pull away when Caril darted across the

yard to the cab. Bob Von Busch said in court, "Her voice was loud, and she seemed to be smiling and crying at the same time. She had her housecoat on and looked awful run-down. Her hair looked like it hadn't been put up for a week. She looked pretty rough. She was awful white."

Caril stood a few feet away from the cab and spoke through the cab window to Barbara: "I'm sorry I was so cranky but I had to be that way."

"Why?" Barbara asked.

"I can't tell you. Just go home and don't come back till after Monday. If you do, things will happen — Mom will get hurt!" She turned and ran back to the house.

Bob and Barbara went home, but Bob got Charlie's brother Rodney and returned that evening. They banged on the front door until Caril finally opened it a few inches. Bob told her he wanted to see Velda, to pay her for some laundry she had done for them. He said that if everybody was sick they could probably use the money. Then he grabbed the door and said he was going to force his way in if he had to. Caril started crying and said, "Please don't try to get in. Mom's life will be in your hands if you do!"

Bob and Rodney wisely decided against going in. Instead, they went to the police. That same evening two officers in a radio car were dispatched to the house. The officers, Donald Kahler and Frank Soukup, later filed a report describing what took place. They went up to the front screen door of the dark house, knocked, and when nobody answered they knocked harder. Then they tried to open the screen but found it hooked. About that time Caril, wearing a kimono and looking sleepy, answered the door and they asked her what the trouble was.

She told them there was no trouble, but that her sister and brother-in-law had come to visit and had not been allowed in because the family had the flu. Doctor's orders. One of the officers told her it seemed strange that her brother-in-law called the police just because of that. She said that Bob didn't like them very much, that "we don't get along too good." The officers wrote in their report that Caril seemed calm, sincere, and gave no reason for them to doubt her. They remarked that a small brown dog — Kim — started jumping on them and Caril opened the screen to let him inside.

After they left the house, they went to a call box on the corner of 10th and Oak and called the station about what had taken place. The captain on duty asked them if they had found out the name of the Bartletts' doctor. They hadn't but said they could go back and find out. The captain said no, it wouldn't be necessary at that time.

Shortly before his recent retirement, Lincoln Police Chief Joe Carroll — one of the more heralded chiefs in the country — sat behind a desk flanked by state and national flags, his short-wave radio playing loudly, and talked about the Starkweather case. After forty-six years in law enforcement, with thirty-four of these as chief, he seemed to have an almost flawless record. He said his department had never had an unsolved murder (though a recent article in the Lincoln *Journal* said there may be as many as seven). He was the fourth recipient of the J. Edgar Hoover Award. Big, powerful, with a crushing hand-shake and booming voice, Carroll became more thoughtful when the name Starkweather was brought up. Despite the criticism the Lincoln Police Department came under because of its handling of the case, Carroll doesn't acknowledge it as a difficult one. "Once we knew who our man was, it was then a matter of putting certain routine procedures into motion. The hard cases are the ones where you have no clues, no motive, no suspect. My biggest worry wasn't Starkweather, it was what the community might do to itself before we caught him." He pulled from his desk a copy of the report made by Harold Robinson, the investigator from California, which vindicates police activities relating to the Starkweather case. "In my view, this report tells the whole story. It's the most complete and accurate piece of writing ever done on Starkweather."

Shortly after the murder of the Bartlett family, Carroll answered reporters as to why the investigators had failed to enter the Bartlett home. "At no time until the discovery of the bodies was there any indication of foul play. We investigate thousands of domestic complaints a month, and this one appeared to be nothing out of the ordinary. We had no legal right to make a forcible entry into the house and no evidence urging us to do so. It is easy to look back now and see what could have been done but we had no knowledge at the time of anything in the nature of a crime. I fail to see any grounds for criticism of the handling of this investigation."

While the two policemen questioned Caril, Bob and Rodney had watched from down the street but had not been able to hear the conversation. Afterward, the two boys went to the police station to find out what happened. They were told nothing was wrong at the Bartletts', except that they had the flu and that people should leave them alone.

One reason the police believed Caril and not Bob, according to Harold Robinson, was because the Von Busches had little credibility with the police. Robinson wrote in his report: "Your investigator had an opportunity to check the files of the Lincoln Police Department with respect to police matters handled in the past relating to the family and relatives of Robert Von Busch. Your investigator was impressed with the number of instances where police attention had been requested on matters arising out of domestic difficulties. Although police officers are admonished not to evaluate the seriousness of an assignment prior to inquiry, it is the writer's conviction that the police officials had an awareness of the number of incidents involving domestic difficulties requiring police action which had occurred in the Von Busch family previously."

Bob Von Busch's response to the statement: "It's ridiculous, just another example of the way the police do things around here. They got me mixed up with Sonny Von Busch and his family. My side of the family never went to the police about anything — and we were never in trouble with the police either."

Though the police had not felt it was necessary to contact the family's doctor, Bob Von Busch did — and he found out the doctor had not seen them. Robinson remarked on this in his report, saying that perhaps under "ideal circumstances of experience and training" the police should have done what common sense told Bob Von Busch to do. But he added that the police did not deserve all the public criticism voiced over the matter; because of Caril's perfect conduct at the door, such interrogation would not necessarily follow.

After leaving the police station in disgust, Bob went home to the rooming house, and Barbara told him that Charlie Starkweather had called twice while he was gone. The first time he called, Charlie said that he had left the .22 he had borrowed from Rodney at the Griggses' and that he was stranded out on Highway 77 at the Tate's service station and needed a ride home. Then he had called back fifteen minutes later and said that the Bartletts all had the flu, that he had taken them groceries, and that everybody should stay away.

Bob called Rodney, who was living at the Starkweather home, and they went together to the Griggses'. Mr. and Mrs. Harvey Griggs said that Charlie had dropped off the gun not long before and, after Charlie left, they had discovered the butt plate missing. Bob and Rodney then drove the eight miles out to Tate's station but Charlie wasn't there, and they were told he hadn't been there. The call had been a ruse to take attention away from the Bartletts'; the boys did not report this new information to the police.

The next morning Rodney showed his father, Guy, the damaged gun, but they decided not to call the police again until they had more evidence. Guy then sent his sixteen-year-old daughter, Laveta, an attractive brunette Charlie liked to draw pictures of, over to see what she could learn. Laveta got along well with Caril, they were confidantes, and Guy felt she might be the one person who could get Caril to tell the truth.

Caril met her at the door and insisted nothing was wrong, everybody just had the flu. Laveta left, then returned later that evening and told Caril that she could tell she wasn't telling the truth and that she wanted to know what was going on in there.

According to Laveta, Caril paused, glanced behind her, then whispered through the screen, "Some guy is back there with Chuck. He has a Tommy gun. I think they're going to rob a bank."

Laveta took the startling information back to her father, who didn't know whether to believe it or not. This was at about seven on Sunday evening. He would not decide to call the police again until the next day.

On Monday morning, Caril's grandmother, sixty-two-year-old Pansy Street, despaired of anyone but herself ever solving the mystery on Belmont Avenue. At about nine-thirty, before going to her job as a fry cook, she took a cab to the Bartletts'. The heavyset woman told the cab driver to wait, and she made her way up the wooden sidewalk to the front door. Ignoring the sign now on the screen — "Stay a way Every Body is sick with The Flue" — she called until Caril answered. Pansy was extremely fond of Caril, but she wasn't about to be lied to by the child. Caril seemed to know it. After telling the flu story, Caril, according to Pansy, suddenly stepped back inside the room, looking pale, and cried, "Go home, Grandma. Oh, Granny, go away! Mommy's life is in danger if you don't."

This made Pansy more determined than ever to see her daughter. Later, in court, she told what she did. "Betty!" she yelled into the house. "You say something so I'll know you're all right!" When no one answered she yelled, "If you can't speak, come to the door! I want to see you!" Nothing. She began to call her little granddaughter. "Betty Jean! Speak to Granny!" Pansy was furious. "Caril, you open this door and let me in! I'm going to get in this house and see what's wrong with Betty. If you don't open this door this second, I'm going to go to town and get a search warrant. You've got Chuck in there with you, and don't try to tell me you don't!"

Caril only stood there.

Pansy got back in the cab and went to the police station. She said later that while she was in the station, talking to an officer, there was a phone call and she overheard the name of Charles Starkweather mentioned. It turned out the call was from Guy Starkweather, who had decided to try to have his son picked up. Pansy was sent to another office and finally two plainclothes men drove her back out to Belmont Avenue. They found the handwritten note on the front door, which was signed "Miss Bartlett." Later, Caril said that she wrote "Miss" instead of "Mrs." to tip off the police that something was wrong.

No one answered the door.

At Pansy's insistence, one of the officers — without a warrant — entered the house through a window and opened the door. A search of the house was made. No one was there. Nothing looked suspicious. The police left, taking Pansy to the tenement house on 10th Street. On the way they told her she should mind her own business and not stick her nose into her children's affairs if they didn't want her around. She said later that she had been far from satisfied with the investigation. The house had been too neat to have had sick people in it. In fact, she was so certain that something had happened that when she went to work at the cafe at eleven she turned on the radio to wait for the bad news. She heard it around six that night.

Harold Robinson made some conclusions concerning the Monday visit to the Bartletts': "In examining the interior of the dwelling it is standard technique for an investigator to look for articles or furniture out of place, upset, damaged or strewn around as an indication they had been ransacked or that some act of violence had taken place. Even acknowledging that some future disarray undoubtedly took place incidental to the search and photographing of the interior of 924 Belmont by police authorities, your investigator asserts that it would be difficult indeed even at this time to resolve the question of whether violence had occurred therein. It is also noted in this connection that according to information given your investigator Charlie and Caril 'cleaned up' the house after removing the bodies of the victims."

Robinson went on to disagree with Pansy Street's contention that she had known something was wrong. He said that she had been perfectly satisfied that everything was normal. The main function of the police, stated Robinson, had been to satisfy Pansy. Once they had done this, duty had been served. This is the explanation he gave for the police not looking in the back yard where the bodies had been for six days: Pansy had not asked them to.

Later that same day, Bob Von Busch paid another visit to the police station and demanded that a more thorough search be made of the premises. He was told there was no reason to make such a search, that the Bartletts had probably gone on vacation. He asked them if they didn't think it strange that a family who had had the five-day flu would suddenly pick up and go on a vacation without telling anyone and, besides that, leave behind a fourteen-year-old daughter? They seemed not to.

Guy Starkweather, in the meantime, had been making continuing efforts to have his son arrested. His call to the station that morning had gotten no results, so he had gone there in person shortly thereafter. Again he got no results, except to have attention called to the fact that he had been drinking. But after the detectives dropped off Pansy, they did go to the Starkweather residence and tell Guy that his son was not at 924 Belmont. In their report, they noted that Guy showed evidence of further drinking since his visit to the station. They also noted that Caril's sister, Barbara, called while they were there. They said that she seemed hysterical because she still did not know where her parents were, despite the fact that their car was still in the yard at 924 Belmont and that Caril had apparently disappeared after Pansy's visit.

Guy later called the police again and said that he had learned that Charlie's car, which had been parked in the Griggses' garage, was now gone. The police went to the garage and determined that the car was indeed gone. They did not, as Guy urged, issue a warrant for his arrest.

It was Bob Von Busch, along with Rodney, who finally found the bodies. The two went back to Belmont around four-thirty Monday afternoon and made a search of the premises. They took one look in the outhouse and, once again, hurried to the police station. This time they were not ignored.

At 5:43 P.M. an alert was issued: "Pick up for investigation, murder, Charles R. Starkweather. May live at 3024 N St., 19 years old. Also pick up Caril A. Fugate, 924 Belmont. Starkweather will be driving a 1949 Ford, black color, license 2-15628. This is a sedan, no grille, and is painted red where the grille was, and has no hub caps."

Chapter FOUR

WHEN THE POLICE had come by the Bartletts' the first time on Saturday night, Charlie had been asleep in Caril's bedroom. Caril was up, watching television. When Nig started barking she peeked out the window, saw the police car, then rushed into the bedroom, crying that the cops were coming. Charlie grabbed a gun and hid in the bathroom, while Caril slipped a nightgown over her clothes and went to the door. After she had talked them out of coming in, Charlie decided to get rid of Rodney's gun and also give the impression that he was across town. He took the gun to the Griggses', a block away, then went to Hutson's where he bought a few items and called Barbara Von Busch with the story about being out at Tate's. He returned to the Bartletts', but — according to Charlie — Caril sent him back to Hutson's a second time to call Barbara and warn her again not to come over.

Caril managed to deal with Laveta on Sunday — or at least

she got rid of her. After Laveta left, Caril and Charlie found a yellow building permit in the house, and Caril wrote on the back of it the note warning people to stay away. She stuck it on the front screen door with bobby pins.

But when Pansy Street came by on Monday morning, Charlie finally decided that they had to leave. He was having breakfast in bed when she arrived; the police found during one of their searches the half-eaten plate of bacon and eggs. Charlie later told Fahrnbruch, "You could hear that old woman yelling all up and down the block. We knew we had to get out fast." He told Caril to pack her things. She didn't have an overnight bag so she filled up the carrying case of her 45 record player. But then she decided it was too big and, instead, put her things in a red swim bag. Included were some snapshots from the family photo album: Betty Jean playing with a plastic tea set at Christmastime; Velda, Barbara, and Caril washing clothes together; Caril and Laveta making faces in a photo booth; Charlie with his shirt open and holding a demolition derby crash helmet against his hip. With the swim bag, the .32 pistol, the hunting knife, and the sawed-off shotgun wrapped in a blue blanket, they slipped out the back way and went down the alley to the Griggses' house to get Charlie's car.

Most of Charlie's hunting trips had been in the countryside around the small town of Bennet, about twenty miles from Lincoln. Usually he had hunted on a farm belonging to seventy-year-old August Meyer, an old friend of the family's. Charlie and the old man got along well, and Charlie always gave him half of everything he shot. He and Caril decided to go there now. In a way, it was what he had always wanted. He had a girl and could be alone in peace with just her and nature. During one of his rambling discourses on nature in his life's story, he wrote that nothing, not even a beautiful model standing posed before him, could satisfy him as much as being out in the woods. He observed that the air is fresher than in the city, has a sweet aroma, and makes one feel revived, reborn. Some people, he knew, would think it lonely in the woods, but it never was for him. Here was a chance to be away from the world of people he hated with such bitterness.

Old Man Meyer? They would have to wait and see about him. But one thing was certain. Never again, until the end, would anybody stop Charlie Starkweather from doing what he wanted.

At the Griggses', he loaded up the car, then discovered he had a flat tire. He sent Caril in to borrow a screwdriver, which he needed to open the trunk, and went to work.

At least one writer, Michael Lydon, saw Charlie as the archetypal teen-ager of the fifties fleeing from the establishment. Lydon wrote in an article called "Wheels on Fire": "The image of Starkweather in Nebraska, flat country frozen in mid-winter, iron ground below and iron sky above, running pressed between two implacabilities toward a horizon which he could never meet — it was simply too much for my imagination to bear . . ." And this image does almost fit Charlie's earlier vision of himself and Caril on the endless open highway. But it was not to turn out that way. The reality was a grim series of aborted starts, mistakes, indecision, and incredible stupidity. It was an expression not of disenchanted youth but rather of terrible poverty of mind and spirit. Lydon wrote: "Flight — just running, getting away — had no moral overtone of weakness; it was instead a necessary act that expressed a major adolescent crisis with dramatic perfection."

But these lines presuppose dignity, reason.

After the tire was changed, they went to the Crest station where they bought a tank of gas and got maps of Nebraska and several adjoining states. Then they drove to the garage Charlie rented on 26th and Woodsdale in the wealthy Country Club section of South Lincoln. He used to collect garbage there, and an older couple, the Southworths, had rented him the space as a favor. Caril waited while Charlie went in the garage and returned with two spare tires. The house on Woodsdale was where her family was supposedly being held hostage.

The wheel Charlie had put on at the Griggses' had a bent rim and the tube was sticking out, making the car shimmy when he went over forty. He was trying to get to Tate's station before going to Bennet to have the tire fixed, but the transmission began to growl so badly that he stopped first at Dale's Champion Service, which was closer. An ex-schoolmate of Charlie's, Lee Lamson, put the car up on the grease rack and packed the transmission — but for some reason did not fix the tire. Caril stayed in the car and drank a Pepsi while Charlie went to the restroom. She later told Fahrnbruch that while she was up on the rack she scribbled a note that said "Help Police — Don't Ignore" and put it in her jacket to give to somebody later. She said she never had a chance to hand it to anybody, but the note was not found in her jacket after their capture.

They proceeded on the bad wheel to Highway 77, past the Nebraska State Penitentiary, and managed to reach Tate's station where they had it fixed. They also bought ammunition, which was commonly sold at service stations in the area, a pair of gloves for Charlie, and got more maps. There was a café adjoining the station and, while Charlie was tending to the car, Caril went to buy hamburgers. The counter girl, Juanita Bell, later remembered the incident vividly in court: "I first saw her out at the pumps, coming toward the café. She was walking fast at first, then started to run. She gave a little smile when she came in. She sat on the stool at the end of the counter and ordered four hamburgers to go. I remember she was wearing a blue jacket, a pink kerchief, and boots. I walked to the door of the kitchen and gave the order to the cook. There were three or

four customers in the café at the time. It took about ten minutes to make the hamburgers. Just as they were ready, Charles
Starkweather came in and handed her a ten-dollar bill, which
she gave to me. He went to the door, which was between the
last booth and the juke box, and waited. After I gave her the
change, she walked over and bumped into him. They talked,
then she gave him a shove as if she wanted to leave in a hurry.
She walked outside and down the sidewalk, looking through the
windows at me until she was out of sight. She had watched me
like that all the time she had been in the café."

Charlie said later to Fahrnbruch that as they left Tate's and
pulled onto the road to Bennet, Caril bit into one of the hamburgers and said, "Ugh. This tastes like dog food. Let's take
them back."

"We're not going back anywhere."

According to Charlie, Caril said, "Well, we ought to. We
ought to go back and shoot them for serving junk like this."

It was now one in the afternoon, three hours after Pansy
Street and the police had learned that Caril was missing from
the Bartlett house. It was one hour since Guy Starkweather had
told the police that Charlie's car was missing from the Griggses'
garage.

To get to August Meyer's farm, which was two miles east of
the tiny farm village of Bennet, they took the main road past the
Bennet cemetery into town, turned east onto a farm road at the
Bennet Community Church, traveled about a mile, then turned
north onto another farm road. Several hundred yards down this
road, on the right, August Meyer's mailbox, bullet-riddled by
hunters, marked the entrance to a narrow tree-lined lane which
went the final mile down to the old man's white two-story
farmhouse. A few days earlier, there had been a six-inch snow-
fall. The snow had by now mostly melted, leaving the lane a
mire of mud and slush. Seconds after pulling onto the lane
they found themselves hopelessly stuck.

It is not known for certain that Charlie planned to kill August Meyer, but the condition of his lane started Charlie and Caril talking about it. Charlie said later, "Caril got pissed off because we got stuck. She said we ought to go up and blast the shit out of him because he didn't shovel his lane. I said it, too. She had my hunting knife, and she said she would let him have it if she got close enough to him."

When Caril was questioned by Fahrnbruch about this she said, "When we got stuck, when we were going out there and got stuck, and couldn't get it out, I think he said he could kill him for it, and I said so could I. And I could. I could, too. Anyway, I mentioned it . . . I was mad because it was cold, and I said I could kill him too."

Forty-five feet north of the lane, and 173 feet east of the main farm road, there had at one time been a small country school. In 1958, there was still debris around, and the storm cellar was still intact. The cellar, common in this tornado country, was no different from many others in the area: the opening, shaped like a large coffin, was close to the ground and surrounded by weeds and a light covering of snow. The heavy wooden door, unhinged but still in place over the entrance, opened to a steep and narrow cement staircase, which went down twelve feet to a circular room eight feet in diameter. The room was cluttered with trash and almost a dozen old wooden school desks. After trying unsuccessfully to get the Ford out of the mud, Charlie and Caril went down in the cellar to rest and get warm. They stayed there about ten minutes, then made the long walk down the lane to the Meyer farm.

Caril's version of what happened when they reached the farm house differs considerably from Charlie's. But whoever was telling the truth, it is difficult to understand how it happened at all. August Meyer was known as a kindly old gentleman, a quiet bachelor who, according to his neighbors, "minded his own business," "kept a neat farm," and who "wouldn't hurt a flea." He had had a long, pleasant relationship with Charlie — ever since Guy Starkweather had first brought Charlie to the farm as a child to go hunting. Charlie was accustomed to staying in the farmhouse when it rained during a hunting trip. He had eaten at the man's table. As recently as November, he and Caril had been there shooting squirrels.

Caril said later, ". . . we walked up and the dog started barking, and Mr. Meyer came out . . . the back door . . . I was following Chuck . . . he was in front of me, walking toward the house . . . Mr. Meyer came out, and I don't know what he said, and then we walked over to the red barn. It was the first barn, and Chuck said he needed the horses to pull the car out . . . and Mr. Meyer said . . . I don't know what he said . . . and then we started to go in the door, and I saw . . . Chuck . . . raise the gun and heard a shot."

Charlie, though, as with all the murders he committed, claimed self-defense. He said that before they went up to the Meyer farmhouse, they went into one of the red barns on the property to warm up. They were in the barn about five minutes, then went up to Meyer's back porch. Meyer's dog was in the yard barking, and Meyer opened the back door and stepped out when Charlie reached the porch. Charlie explained to the farmer that they were stuck and needed a horse to pull the car out. "I got into a helluva argument with Meyer," Charlie said later. "He couldn't understand why I got stuck there. He thought we should have gotten stuck up closer to his house." Charlie went on to say that Meyer said he was going in to get his coat, but that he wouldn't let them come in the house to get warm. He told them to go into the washhouse instead. Then, according to Charlie, the old man reappeared on the porch with a rifle and took a shot at him: "I felt the bullet go by my head." Charlie claimed that Mr. Meyer tried to shoot again but his gun jammed, and he turned to go back inside. "Meyer started running back in the house, and I shot him." Charlie had been standing about five feet from the porch, but he went up the steps and shot the farmer in the head at almost pointblank range with the sawed-off .410. Unless Charlie somehow gave away what he had done, it is hard to believe Mr. Meyer would take a shot at him over an argument about Charlie's car being stuck. It does seem possible, though, that Mr. Meyer could have appeared on the porch with a gun and Charlie, frightened and paranoid, *thought* he was going to shoot and so decided to shoot first. At any rate, it was very important to Charlie that the authorities believe his motive for killing the farmer. When he told his version to Chief Deputy Fahrnbruch, the deputy said, "Okay, Caril doesn't tell me that."

"Caril doesn't tell you a lot of things."

"I know that. I'm not trying to argue with you or anything. I just want you to tell me the truth."

"I'll argue with you all night about that. I got more sleep than you have."

For the most part, their stories corresponded concerning what happened after the murder. Charlie dragged the body about fifty feet out to the washhouse and covered it up inside with a white blanket. Caril tossed Mr. Meyer's hat in the little shed, and they closed the door. As they were about to return to the house, Mr. Meyer's dog came to within about thirty feet of them, barking, and Charlie shot him. The wounded dog went off across the pasture, in the direction of a creek which ran through the property.

Back at the house, Charlie spread some throw rugs over the pool of blood on the porch, and they went inside to get warm, eat, and search for money and weapons. The farmhouse was typical of the better farms in the area — a spartan and solidly built two-story frame with a total of eight small rooms. A porch extended around most of the house. Inside, the green wallpaper had a leaf design, and the doors and woodwork were the color of dark mahogany. Besides a few gilt-framed pictures of relatives from another time, the farmer had no ornaments on the walls. What furniture he had was built to last forever and from the design gave the appearance of having already been passed down for several generations. There was no electricity in the house, and all the rooms had gas-burning lamps. There was a pump organ in the living room, and in one bedroom was an old Victrola with a hand crank. A gas stove heated the kitchen.

Caril told Fahrnbruch how they spent part of the time in the house: "We went in . . . the kitchen . . . I sat down by the stove there, and then he got up and went upstairs. He was looking for a gun . . . he came down and looked through the downstairs, and I kept looking out the window . . . to see if anyone was coming . . . then he came out with the guns, three of them . . . two great big ones, and there was a .22, and then . . . we went in the kitchen. I went in there and sat down. He was looking for some money. Some people gave Mr. Meyer some money, he said. He had about $500 in the house. Then he said Mr. Meyer had a lot of clothes, brand new clothes he just bought, and he went in the other room, and I went in there too . . . he got two pairs of socks and a big jacket and two pairs of white gloves . . . there should be a pair of white gloves in my black coat . . . he told me to put a pair of socks on but I wouldn't."

Caril went on to say that Charlie put on clean socks, throwing his old ones on the floor, then he searched for and found some money — not nearly as much as he had hoped — in a brown pouch. He found some Jell-O and cookies to eat, but Caril refused to have any. She said, "He stuck his finger in it and said the Jell-O was good. I kept saying, 'Let's go,' because I was scared." Her explanation for being afraid seems strange if

verse then," he said later. ". . . And I couldn't turn because my front wheels was in a rut . . . So I went down in this guy's corn field and went back up. Boy, you ought to have seen the corn fly there — stalks and everything flying behind me."

When they had been to Tate's station earlier, the owner, Homer Tate, had thought the couple seemed peculiar. Charlie had insisted on parking his car out of sight of the highway, and Tate noticed the butt of a shotgun sticking out from under a blanket in the front seat beside Caril. Though he took note of these things, they didn't seem significant enough to act upon. When Charlie and Caril got off the dead-end road and found their way back to Tate's the second time, a Tate station attendant, Marvin Krueger, was on duty. He sensed right away that something was going on. There were two guns in the front seat, the barrels in Caril's lap, two spare tires in the back seat — they had acquired a total of six extra tires — and Charlie asked for two boxes of .22 shells, hollow point. It was now about five-thirty and getting dark, an odd time to be buying shells, and Krueger jotted down Charlie's license number. He later called the information into the police but, even though the pickup order had been issued by then, no one followed through on the lead.

Now that they were away from the Meyer farm, Charlie decided they had been hasty to run off as they did. The fact that the blanket was missing from over Meyer's body didn't necessarily mean anything. The wind could have blown it off. Even though the door and window of the washhouse were closed, the wind was blowing hard enough to perhaps have caused a strong draft under the door. Caril went into Tate's and got a map of Kansas because, she said, "Chuck wanted them to think we were going to Kansas," and they drove back to the Meyer farm to spend the night.

But as they were driving up the passable lane to the farmhouse, Caril demanded that Charlie stop. She had a premonition that somebody was there, that the body had been found. After all, it had been uncovered, in plain sight, ever since they left. Charlie said later that it was partly the body itself she was afraid of. "She thought he was going to get back up and sit there waiting for us." But then he lost his nerve, too, and they decided to leave. When Charlie tried to turn the car around, he got stuck again.

It was completely dark now and so cold they couldn't try to get the car out again, so they took their weapons and walked back down the lane to the country road. Lights from warm farmhouses glowed in the distance, and Caril wanted to go up to one of them. Charlie refused. "There's too many of them farmers," he said. "We'll spend the night in the cave."

They were walking down the road in the direction of the storm cellar when a car rounded a bend and caught them in its headlights. Charlie hesitated, shifted his rifle to his left hand, and stuck out his thumb.

Bennet, Nebraska, population around 400, has always been an easy town to miss. Its biggest landmark is its cemetery. In 1958, the downtown area, off the main road through town, was a single block of small stores reminiscent of Old West movie props. The post office and Jensen's General Store were the main places of business. Some of the other stores over the years had boarded up their windows. Bennet has always been quiet, somber, almost ghostly.

Jensen's General Store, even in 1958, was anachronistic, a little wooden-floored grocery with a meat counter and four or five rows of food — mostly canned goods and a wide assortment of candy for the local children who trailed in and out throughout the day. The owner, Robert Jensen, heavy-jowled and stolid, usually stood behind the meat counter in a spotted white apron, talking laconically with locals about the crops and weather. He had been there much of his life, defying surrounding decline and the giant Lincoln supermarket chains. It almost seemed as if Bennet could turn to dust and Jensen's General Store would somehow survive, somehow stay OPEN FOR BUSINESS. The fervent attachment of its owner to the area, its people, his store used to be stated on the back of his bills of sale:

Little Town

I like to live in a little town
   where the trees meet across the street
Where you wave your hand and say "Hello"
   to everyone you meet.

I like to stand for a moment
   outside the grocery store
And listen to the friendly gossip of
   the folks that live next door.

For life is interwoven
   with the friends we learn to know
And we hear their joys and sorrows
   as we daily come and go.

So I like to live in a little town
   I care no more to roam.

For every home in a little town
   is more than a house, it's home.

Late Monday afternoon Robert Jensen's seventeen-year-old son, Bob Junior, got out of school and went to the grocery store to work until he and his father closed up at six. Bob was a big boy — six feet tall and 240 pounds — and a year before at this time of the day he had been over at the high school playing football. But the aftereffects of having polio as a child finally forced him to give up athletics. Getting out of sports left him more time to help his father and to see his girlfriend, Carol

King. The young couple were engaged now and, since the
death of her father only three weeks before, he saw her almost
every evening. They lived only half a block apart — just down
the street from the store — and usually visited at each other's
home to watch TV and talk with their families. They were a
model couple, the most popular at the high school, and were
the opposites of Charlie and Caril. Bob and Carol saw nothing
wrong with the world, nothing major to rebel against. They
were happy to be reproductions of their parents and had never
been alienated from anything. They both were good students,
sang in the school and church choirs, belonged to the Church
Youth Fellowship, and went to Bible school during the summer. Their high school yearbook pictures made them seem be-
nign and placid, and they looked more like adults than high
school kids. Yet they did not have a holier-than-thou attitude;
they were still teen-agers with whims and passions, and were as
subject to fads as anybody else their age. Carol was a slender,
attractive brunette who was both a cheerleader and a majorette.
Bob might have had short hair and preferred a school letter
jacket to a motorcycle jacket, but he still had loud mufflers on
his 1950 Ford. In his billfold he secretly carried a couple of
French postcards and a crudely typed list of obscene sayings attributed to Confucius. And when he and Carol wanted to be
alone, they took long drives down the lonely country roads to
the local parking spots used by Bennet teen-agers.

After the store was locked up that day, Bob delivered a half
gallon of milk to a neighbor, then went home to eat and to call
Carol to see if she wanted to go out. He spoke with his father
in their basement den, getting the go-ahead to buy two recapped
tires for his car. Bob Senior asked him to pick up some American Legion membership cards at the local adjutant's house, saying he could just hold on to the cards until he came home from
his evening with Carol.

86

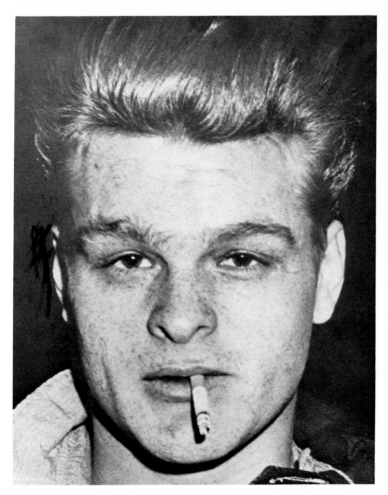

Charles Starkweather strikes a James Dean pose for a mug
shot taken after his capture.

Caril Fugate and Charlie, taken by his landlady only
months before the murder spree.

Charlie's parents, Guy and Helen Starkweather, confer.

Caril's stepfather, Marion Bartlett, drapes a chivalrous arm around the shoulder of her mother, Velda.

A family snapshot shows Caril's half sister, Betty Jean Bartlett, enjoying her last Christmas.

Robert Colvert, the night attendant at the Crest service station outside Lincoln, Nebraska, was Charlie's first victim.

After murdering the Bartletts, Charlie holed up with Caril for six days at her house at 924 Belmont Avenue in Lincoln.

Caril's puppy, Kim, abandoned at the Bartlett residence. The sign, put up by its mistress, reads: "Stay away Every Body is sick with The Flue."

Charlie left behind two shotguns (but took a .22 pump rifle) in the ransacked house of his fifth victim, farmer August Meyer.

Class of 1958: Carol King and Robert Jensen, in their high school yearbook pictures.

The body of Robert Jensen, shot six times in the head, lies amid old school desks in an abandoned storm cellar.

Lawmen remove the corpse of Carol King from the Bennet, Nebraska, storm cellar.

Charlie's 1949 Ford, stuck in the mud by the lane to the Meyer farm.

Three more bodies were found in the home of industrialist C. Lauer Ward, in the Country Club section of Lincoln.

Clara Ward

C. Lauer Ward

Lillian Fencl

Lancaster County sheriff Merle Karnopp (l.) leads a smirking Charlie Starkweather to his trial.

Rebel without a cause: even in the shadow of the electric chair, Starkweather pursued the James Dean image.

Starkweather, who yearned for the solitude of the wilderness, did this sketch in prison.

In the back of the police car taking her to Lincoln, Caril
sips a bottle of Pepsi.

Caril Fugate today, in her room at
the women's reformatory in York,
Nebraska.

At the King house down the street, Carol helped fix supper and sat down to eat with her mother and older brother, Warren. She showed them her report cards, which had come out that day, and they were not surprised that she had made perfect marks again. She always was the best student in her class. After dinner, she helped with the dishes and sat down to study. Then Bob called and she got permission to go for a short ride. She promised to be in by ten.

Bob picked up the membership cards, then went to the Bennet gas station, charged three dollars' worth of gas, ordered his new tires, and drove straight to the King house. Carol met him at the door wearing jeans and a sweat shirt. He waited on the porch for the few seconds it took her to put on a scarf and a heavy tan winter coat, then they were off for a few precious minutes alone.

The lane between the bridge and the railroad tracks leading up to Meyer's farm was a favorite parking place for local teenagers. It was secluded and had no traffic at all, except perhaps for other parking couples. Sometimes three or four cars would be on the lane at the same time. This night, though, was a week night, and the weather and roads were bad. The road leading to the lane was deserted except for Charlie and Caril, who walked along, hunched with cold, carrying Meyer's .22 pump and Marion Bartlett's sawed-off .410.

When the couple appeared in Bob's headlights, he must have debated briefly whether to help them. It would cut into his time alone with Carol. And it could be risky: the couple was armed. But Bob had a reputation for being considerate, and in a farm community like Bennet it was impolite to pass up someone in trouble. Also, because of the conversation which follows, authorities speculated that he had seen the redheaded boy in the area before, that he remembered the boy had a Ford, one not unlike his own, except that Bob's had whitewall tires, twin antennae on the rear fenders, and was in better condition.

According to Charlie, Bob pulled to a stop, rolled down his window, and said, "Is there any trouble?"

"Yeah," Charlie said. "Our car's stuck and we've got a gear out."

Bob studied Charlie a moment, trying to place him. "You own a Ford, don't you?"

"Yeah."

"Black? 1949?"

"Yeah."

"Get in. We'll give you a lift to town."

Charlie and Caril were climbing in the back seat when Bob turned around and took hold of the barrel of Charlie's gun, the .22 pump. "I'll take these, okay?"

"What for?" Charlie asked. "They ain't loaded."

"We don't walk around with loaded guns," Caril said.

This seemed to satisfy Bob, and he drove on toward Bennet.

On the way, Charlie became suspicious that Bob knew who they were and what they had done. Otherwise how did he know what kind of car they had? Why would he ask for their guns if he didn't suspect something?

Charlie told Bob to take them to a pay phone. According to Charlie's testimony at Caril's trial, he was toying with the idea of calling his "buddy," Sheriff Karnopp, who had once lived across the street from him, and turning himself in. But it occurred to him that if he did, Bob Jensen might get the credit for their capture. Charlie wasn't about to let the story get around that this fat kid had caught him and Caril. Nobody was going to be a hero at his expense.

According to Charlie, they pulled into the closed Bennet service station and Bob said, "There's the phone booth but it's locked up. I'll get the guy with the key to open it for you."

Charlie gave up all pretense and put the rifle against the back of Bob's head. "Oh, no, you ain't. You better do what we tell you before somebody gets hurt!" According to Caril, Charlie's voice was "scared and shaky, squeaky kind of like — loud and squeaky."

"What do you want?" Bob asked.

Charlie told him to drive them to Lincoln.

They were on State Highway 2 to the city when Charlie changed him mind and ordered Bob to drive to the school cellar.

"What are you going to do with us?"

"Nothing. Leave you there."

"Are you going to take my car?"

"Yeah."

"Well, try not to burn it up. And be careful about the drive shaft when you go over a bump."

According to Charlie, Caril turned to him and said, "Have you asked the boy for his money yet?"

He told Bob to pass back his billfold. Caril took the money out of it, put the bills in Charlie's billfold, and handed Bob's billfold to Carol King. They did not ask Carol if she had any money; they assumed she didn't, since most girls there generally did not pay their own way on dates.

Carol hadn't spoken since Charlie had put the gun on them but when she took the billfold back for Bob, she said, "I want to thank you for not being mean to us."

According to Charlie, Caril snapped, "Shut up!"

"Listen," Bob said. "You won't shoot us, will you?"

"I will if you don't do what I say," Charlie said.

"You've got to be kidding," Bob answered.

Caril said, "If you don't watch it, I'll shoot her and show you if we're kidding or not." Caril later denied saying that, or suggesting they rob Jensen. At her trial she admitted taking money from Bob's billfold and even holding a gun on the couple, but she insisted she did it at Charlie's command.

They drove down the lane to Meyer's farm and parked about

fifty feet from the storm cellar. Caril waited in the car, listening to the radio, while Charlie marched them over to the cellar and down the steps.

County Attorney Elmer Scheele contended in court that as Bob was going down the steps, Charlie ruthlessly shot him from behind. Charlie claimed that Bob went on down the steps but then as Carol was about to follow, Bob came running back up, shoved his girlfriend to one side, and lunged for the gun. He supposedly lost his balance, turned, and Charlie shot him six times in a four-inch area around the left ear. That was Charlie's explanation of how he could have shot the boy from behind and still claim self-defense.

Charlie's early statement to Scheele said that Carol King began screaming and he shot her. This conforms with Caril's story that she hadn't at that time left the car and that she heard shots coming from the cellar but didn't see anything. A later letter from Charlie to Scheele, however, said he didn't shoot Carol King. He said he made her go down in the cellar, where Bob's body had fallen. He was about to cover the door with heavy debris from the razed schoolhouse when he changed his mind and went down himself. He wanted to see if Bob was dead. He said the boy was sitting up at first but soon toppled over. Charlie watched him for about fifteen minutes, until he stopped breathing, then Caril supposedly came over from the car, furious. She thought Charlie was sexually attacking the girl. He went up the stairs, they had what he termed "bloody talk," then, as they started to leave, they got stuck again. He said he left Caril to guard Carol King outside the cellar while he tried to get the car out of the mud. He was jacking up the car, preparing to put boards under the wheel, when a single shot rang out. When he got back to the cellar, Caril was standing beside the body of Carol King. Caril told him she had no choice: the girl had tried to run. Charlie said for her to wait in the car while he took Carol down into the cellar.

The exact sequence of events in and around the cellar that night is vague, but the results were grimly clear when a farmer opened the cellar door the next day. Bob's body, fully clothed, was lying at the bottom of the stairs in a pool of blood. Carol's body, partly nude, was lying on top of his, her coat pulled over her head. Her blue jeans and panties were down around her ankles, and she was streaked with blood and mud from her waist to halfway down her thighs. She had been stabbed several times in the groin. One of the wounds extended through the wall of the cervix into the rectum. An autopsy, made partly to determine if she had also been the victim of a sexual attack, was inconclusive — meaning only that no sperm was found. The findings in the report were those of a bullet wound entering the right side of the head below the ear, causing fractured obstruction of the brain and death. The gunshot had come from behind. There were brush marks, or brush burns along the back, running along the midline of the back, from the level of the lower ribs to the sacrum, as if derived from contact with a rough surface while being dragged. There was copious bleeding from the vagina because of internal damage, and the wound in the cervix, leading into and around the rectum, was made by an undetermined sharp instrument. The instrument could not have been Charlie's hunting knife. The penetrating wound was no more than three quarters of an inch in width and at least three inches deep. Charlie's knife could not have made an incised, sharp pointed wound on both sides and be so narrow in width. The stiletto-type instrument used was never found.

Charlie was reluctant to talk about the sexual aspect of the murder. He denied completing a sexual attack on the girl and claimed that Caril had mutilated her out of jealousy.

Chief Deputy Fahrnbruch later asked Charlie what took place after Bob stopped breathing.

"Temptation."

"What did you do?"

"Well, I pulled her jeans down, but I didn't screw her."

"What did you do to her?"

"Nothing."

"Charlie, you told the officers different, haven't you?"

"I didn't screw her . . . I couldn't get to the point . . . it was colder than hell . . . I left her lay there and left . . . I didn't screw her. I'll argue that with you all night, too."

Charlie, however, had told an officer, Lieutenant Robert Henninger, that he had had sexual relations with Carol King. Henninger was present while Fahrnbruch was questioning Charlie, and at one point Charlie turned to him and said, "You can get all your notes out here."

Fahrnbruch said, "Why, what's he got in his notes?"

"I don't know."

"Well, he's got what you told him."

"Yes."

"Well, what did you tell him?"

"I told him I screwed the shit out of that King girl."

"You also told him that you went in the rear end?"

"No."

"Well, didn't you screw her?"

"No. I didn't do nothing to her."

Charlie insisted that the only reason he ever claimed to have had sexual relations with the King girl was to cover up what Caril had done to her.

Fahrnbruch then directed his questions to what happened after Charlie returned to the car. "Did Caril leave the car then?"

"A couple of times, yes . . . she was pissed off anyway . . . she just called me a dirty bastard and all sorts of things."

"Why did she call you that? Did you do something in that cave that she might have seen?"

"Well, she might have come up to that cave and thought, but I wasn't."

"As a matter of fact you asked her for sexual relations?"

"Yes, but I never got them."

"What did she say?"

"I already had mine for the night . . . she probably walked up there and seen me down there . . . she could have guessed."

"What could she have guessed?"

"What I was doing."

"What did you do?"

"I didn't do nothing."

After the murders, Charlie and Caril covered the door of the cellar with rubbish, then went to work getting Bob's car out of the mud, putting boards and a blanket under the wheels. Around ten-thirty they got out and roared down the lane, onto the farm road to town.

Their loud exit was heard by a neighboring farmer, Everett Broening. He said that the same car had turned around earlier in his driveway. "I have a boy that's about the same age as Jensen, and Jensen's car is equipped with pipes, and if you know boys, they know each other's pipes and how they go up the road, because the boy said, 'There goes Jensen's car,' And I said, 'How come?' Because he always blowed the horn when he went by, and that time he didn't blow it." Later, when the couple were reported missing, Broening remembered hearing the car that night and began a search of the area which led to the discovery of the bodies.

Charlie said that once they were away from the murder site, he told Caril he wanted them to give themselves up. The killing was getting on his nerves. He was tired of running. "She kept trying to talk me out of it," he said later. "We was going down shooting on the highway. I told her I was going to give myself up and she said no I wasn't. I said yes I was and she said no I wasn't." When asked how the argument turned out, he said, "When you got the .410 setting there I wasn't going to do it." He admitted that while the gun was in her lap, facing in his direction, she wasn't aiming at him. "But she said that she wasn't giving herself up and wasn't going to let anything stand in her way. That was good enough for me."

They got on State Highway 2 and headed back to Lincoln, where the search for them was most intense. Charlie could not resist returning to the Bartletts' to see if the bodies of Caril's family had been discovered. They hadn't yet heard the news on the radio. On the way Caril hurled three books belonging to Bob Jensen out the window, scattering them along the highway. Later she said that was one of her tips to the police. They drove right through the center of Lincoln, past the police station, not worried because they were in Jensen's car. A number of police cars were around the Bartletts' house when they arrived and Charlie kept driving.

They headed west out of town. Charlie's brother Leonard was living in the state of Washington, and one of their plans had been to go live with him. For almost three hours they sped nonstop down the highway, reaching the vicinity of Hastings, Nebraska.

Then, incredibly, they turned around and headed back for Lincoln. Charlie said later that he had been too tired to go on, he had to get some rest. The car wasn't running well either, and he thought it would be easier to pick up another one in Lincoln. "I wasn't worried," he said. "I knew the cops wouldn't be expecting us to be coming in from that direction."

Chapter FIVE

CHARLIE AND CARIL arrived in Lincoln about three-thirty in the morning, drove to the wealthy Country Club section of town, and parked near the corner of 24th and Van Dorn — almost in sight of the house on Woodsdale where Caril's parents supposedly were being held. They slept in the car until past dawn.

When they awoke they drove around the area for a while, trying to select a house to hide out in and rob. They planned to steal a car from whatever place they chose and leave that night. Charlie knew who owned some of the wealthy estates in the area — he had collected their garbage — and as they drove around he pointed out a number of possibilities to Caril. He indicated a beautiful two-story white house, set back among trees on a large lot on South 24th, and, according to Charlie in his statement to Scheele, she nodded and told him that that was the one.

The mansion they selected belonged to forty-seven-year-old

industrialist, C. Lauer Ward, president of both the Capital Bridge Company and the Capital Steel Company. Mr. Ward was one of the most respected and influential men in Lincoln. He was a graduate of the University of Nebraska, had attended Harvard and the University of Chicago, and was a member of the Nebraska Bar. He was a millionaire and a good friend of the governor's. His forty-six-year-old wife, Clara, was also a graduate of the University of Nebraska and was vice president of the Nebraska Alumni Association — the highest position a woman could hold in that organization. The couple were prominent in civic and church activities. They had one child, Michael, age fourteen, who was away at a private school in Choate, Connecticut, and there was only one other person living in the house with them at the time: Fifty-one-year-old Lillian Fencl, the maid at the Ward residence for twenty-six years, was considered a member of the family. Also occupying the large house were a Chesapeake Bay retriever named Queenie, who had never been trained to retrieve, and Suzy, a small black poodle who was Mrs. Ward's lap dog.

Charlie had never collected the Wards' garbage — they were on the Von Busches route — but he had collected on nearby streets and had done odd jobs in the area. Less than two weeks before, he and several other boys had shoveled snow from sidewalks along the Wards' street. Bob Von Busch is convinced Charlie knew the Wards' maid and had occasionally stopped in when the Wards weren't home to warm up and get a bite to eat. At any rate, the Ward home was just a minute's walk away from the rented garage where he worked on his hot rod.

The driveway to the Ward mansion circled around the back of the house to a double garage. There was also a rear access drive to the garage, and neighbors often didn't know when the Wards came and went, or when they had visitors. Charlie drove up to the garage at about eight-thirty and pulled partway into the vacant stall left by Mr. Ward, who had gone to work only a few minutes before. Charlie told Caril to wait in the car, and he went, with a rifle, through the garage to the kitchen door and banged on it.

Lillian Fencl, who was deaf, must have seen Charlie through a window in the door and opened it for him. On the kitchen table behind her was the morning Lincoln *Star* with a banner headline reading BELMONT FAMILY SLAIN. A smaller headline said DAUGHTER, BOYFRIEND SOUGHT FOR QUESTIONING, but apparently the maid didn't make the connection.

Charlie didn't bother to speak when she answered the door — he just pointed the gun at her and walked into the kitchen. The dogs began barking and Lillian took Queenie, the large Chesapeake, by the collar and held her. "Put that dog in the basement," Charlie told her, but the maid misunderstood and put Queenie in a nearby bathroom instead. When she returned he tried to talk to her, to tell her what he wanted, but couldn't make her understand. Finally he wrote a note, telling her to sit down and shut up. She did, and he wrote another one asking who else was in the house. She said that Mrs. Ward was upstairs and would soon be down to eat. Breakfast was in preparation on the stove. "Go on and fix it," Charlie said, indicating the stove, and sat down at the kitchen table to watch her and wait.

Mrs. Ward came down in her robe and nightgown about ten minutes later, and Charlie ordered her to sit down at the table. She looked at the newspaper, looked at Charlie, and said nothing.

"You don't have to worry," Charlie said. "Nothing's going to happen. We're going to stay here till night, then we're going to tie you up and leave."

According to Charlie's statement to Scheele, Mrs. Ward said, "All right. That will be okay. You can trust us. You don't have to hold the gun on us or anything like that."

Charlie went to the door and waved for Caril to come inside.

He called for her to bring in the shotgun and his leather jacket, which had ammunition in the pockets. Caril soon appeared, seeming half-asleep, and Mrs. Ward gave her a cup of coffee. Caril took it into the library, drank it alone, then lay down on the couch and went to sleep.

For a while Charlie stayed in the kitchen with the two women, allowing the maid to bring up an ironing board from the basement and iron by the kitchen table. Mrs. Ward said that she had an engagement at eleven that morning for a church "coffee," and Charlie told her to call and say she didn't feel well. She did, then asked if she could do some of her house cleaning. He said that would be all right and he watched while she waxed a large dining room table in the front of the house. Then she went back in the kitchen and began cleaning out the refrigerator.

Charlie got bored watching the women and took a radio from the kitchen into the living room and listened to the newsmen say his name over the air. He spent two or three hours in the elegant living room and other parts of the house, inspecting everything, testing the fine furniture. Reinhardt later quoted Charlie as saying, "You don't think I just sit around in that mansion on my ass, do you?" Around eleven, he decided he wanted breakfast and ordered Mrs. Ward to serve him pancakes in the library. Then he decided he would rather have waffles, so she made those for him instead. He ate six. "They was real nice to us," Reinhardt quoted Charlie. "And I took it while I had it. I knowed it couldn't last long."

It lasted until the early afternoon. The following statement, made to County Attorney Elmer Scheele, is one of the few confessions that Charlie made which wasn't later changed.

". . . about one o'clock Mrs. Ward said she'd like to go upstairs and change her shoes . . . I told her that she could . . . she was up there about forty-five minutes . . . I went on up

98

stairs to see what was keeping her . . . earlier that morning I asked her if they had any guns in the house and she says the only guns they had was a BB gun . . . That afternoon I walked upstairs and she took a shot at me."

Scheele asked, "Where were you when she took a shot at you?"

"To the hallway and about five feet south of her . . . And she just stepped out of the boy's room and she toook a shot at me with the .22 . . . she was standing either in the room or right in the doorway in that room right above the library."

"Did that shot strike you?"

"No . . . I didn't see a thing about it . . . she ran on by me . . . she started going for the top of the steps . . . I had the knife . . . I threw the knife at her . . . It stuck to her back . . . she was moaning and groaning . . ."

"Did she fall?"

"Halfway . . . I just caught her . . . underneath the arms . . . she wasn't all the way to the floor . . . I dragged her into her bedroom . . . she was still talking to me, she wasn't dead . . . I laid her on her bed and just left her there."

"What did you do with the knife?"

"I — I pulled it. I pulled it out . . . I run on down the stairs and Caril was awake then, and I gave her a gun . . . I told her to go in and watch the maid."

"What did you do then?"

"I ran back upstairs . . . I was going to put a Band-Aid or something on there to keep her from bleeding . . . I walked in there and she was trying to get to the phone, so I moved the phone . . . in the outside of the room there."

"Then what did you do?"

"After that I hit the dog . . . She had a dog there . . . A black one . . . I couldn't get near . . . It was trying to bite my hand off . . . Well, I picked up the .22 and he stood up and started barking, and I hit him with it . . . Why, I hit him just like it was a baseball bat . . . with the butt end . . . He just rolled over, and I think I busted his neck . . . he didn't move at all."

"Then what did you do?"

"Well, I put the rope around her, or I took a sheet and cut the sheet and put a piece of sheet around her mouth and hands . . . after that I bound her feet and hands and covered her up."

"What did you cover her with?"

"A blanket."

Around the same time Charlie was attacking Mrs. Ward and her miniature poodle, about twenty-five officers from the Lancaster County sheriff's office, the Nebraska Safety Patrol, and the Lincoln City Police were converging on August Meyer's farm, twenty miles away. Charlie's Ford had been discovered stuck in the mud on Meyer's lane, and one officer thought he had seen someone near the farm, so authorities were convinced they had Charlie trapped in the Meyer house. Newsmen had arrived and a radio bulletin went over the air that the capture would probably take place just as soon as tear gas guns arrived from Lincoln. The police said they weren't sure if Caril Fugate was holed up in the house with Charlie or not.

By the time the tear gas arrived, about thirty armed farmers had also surrounded the farmhouse. Assistant Lincoln Police Chief Eugene Masters called to the house through a loudspeaker: "We know you're in there. We'll give you five minutes to come out with your hands up." After the time passed, nine officers moved within range and fired nine tear gas bombs through the windows. They waited. No one came out. The officers, flanked by the farmers, moved in on the house but so much tear gas had been set off that it was impossible to go inside immediately. While they were waiting for the air to clear, one state trooper, Gerald Tesch, approached the house from the rear, kicked open the small white washhouse, and found August Meyer's body.

Farmer Everett Broening, who was on the scene, then recalled hearing the Jensen car accelerating at high speed away from the razed school down the road the night before. The Bennet teen-agers had by now been reported missing, so on a hunch he walked down the lane and looked inside the cellar. He hurried back to the farm and reported to Sheriff Karnopp what he had found.

A large number of state troopers — estimates went as high as 100 — soon arrived in Bennet from Omaha, Columbus, Grand Island, and Fremont, and began a systematic search of the bleak rolling countryside. Bennet farmers formed into a posse, bought all the ammunition in the local hardware store, and began to search. Bennet residents who didn't join the hunt stayed inside their homes with weapons at their sides.

The search was still under way in Lincoln, and the city was getting more and more anxious, but some authorities thought the couple probably weren't there. If they weren't hiding out in the Bennet area, they were no doubt out of the state by now. After seeing Carol King's body, some felt sure they were dealing with a sex killer and that Caril Fugate had probably met the same fate. Despite this, County Attorney Elmer Scheele had filed charges against her, along with Charlie, for first-degree murder. Descriptions were released:

"*Starkweather* — Five feet five inches tall. 150 pounds. Scar over right eye. Green eyes. Dark red hair cut short on top, long on sides and back. Bowlegged and pigeon-toed, swaggers when he walks. Believed wearing bluejeans and black leather motorcycle jacket, black boots or cowboy boots. Sometimes has speech impediment, trouble pronouncing W's and R's.

"*Caril Fugate* — Five feet one inch tall. 105 pounds.

Looks about 18. Blue eyes. Dark brown hair usually worn in pony tail. Sometimes wears glasses, possibly wearing ring with red setting. Dressed in jeans and blouse or sweater, may be wearing a medium blue parka. Might have on white baton boots or gray suede loafers."

About the middle of the afternoon, Charlie's brother Rodney found Bob Von Busch and gave him a message from Guy Starkweather. Guy said Charlie had called and said that he had left town, but was coming back to Lincoln to kill Bob. He would be coming in on Route Six, which turns into O Street in Lincoln. Today Bob says, "There's no way to prove if Guy was telling the truth or not. Looking back, I can see how he might have made it up, but I never even questioned it at the time." Charlie wasn't asked later if he actually made the call, but it should be noted that Route Six is the highway to Hastings, where he and Caril had been the night before.

Charlie was no longer speaking to his one-time best friend. He believed Bob was trying to break him and Caril up so Caril could go with another friend of Bob's. Judging from mention of Bob in letters written during and after the murder spree, Charlie also was mad at him for pestering them at the Bartletts'. The letter addressed "for the law only," written by Charlie but assuming both his and Caril's points of view, says in part: "then ne and chuck live with each other and nonday the day the bodys were found, we were going to kill our selves but BOB VON BRUCK and everybody would not stay a way . . . and [I] hate ny older sister and bob for what they are they all ways wanted ne to stop going with chuck snow that sone Kid bob Kwen [knew] would go with ne . . . i feel sorry for Bar, to have a ask [ass] like bob. I and Caril are sorry for what has happen, cause i have hurt every body cause of it and so has caril. but i'n saying one thing every body that cane out there was luckie there not *dead* even caril's sister."

Amazingly enough, Bob's reaction to the threat was to go with Rodney to the old O Street viaduct, one of the vantage points in town, and wait for Charlie's arrival. Today, asked why, after his life had been threatened, he would set himself up like a clay pigeon, he shrugs and says, "We figured we didn't have that much to lose, I guess. Anyway, it was two against one. We didn't think he would start shooting right away — he would want to talk first, and when he did we were going to jump him."

Bob and Rodney stood shivering on the bridge most of the afternoon, surveying the town. The city of slightly over 100,000, growing as if for no reason out of the frozen Nebraska plains, seemed on that day almost as barren as the surrounding countryside. The widespread terror Charlie was to create had already begun. O Street cuts a wide swath through the center of town and normally is heavy with traffic — or, with the slightest provocation, an endless procession of baton twirlers, high school bands, Shriners in trick cars, state and local officials, mounted police, the National Guard. These parades seem to make a show of force: *We value what we have and we intend to protect it.* But now two teen-agers, with ease, were driving most of the population inside their homes.

West of the viaduct the plain country stretches toward Wyoming, segmented by country roads cut as straight as city blocks, dotted with white houses, red barns, silos; a mile or so to the south, on the edge of town, looms the gray stone walls and guard towers of the Nebraska State Penitentiary; to the east-northeast is the University of Nebraska campus, "Home of Big Red"; and due east is the downtown area — for the most part a few blocks of squat brick buildings, the streets neatly numbered north and south, alphabetized east and west. But jutting up from among the stores and offices, rising over everything, is the state capitol building, 440 feet high and capped by a gold dome. Perched on top of the dome is a nineteen-feet-high statue of a man scattering seed: the Sower. Often such dominant and inescapable structures — like the Texas tower on the University of Texas campus — have grim histories, seeming to attract murder, accident, suicide. Lincoln's capitol building doesn't seem to have that effect. The standard joke is that it looks like a giant phallus sowing wild oats.

Charlie did not come down O Street during the time Bob made himself so available. As evening came on and the temperature dropped, the boys relinquished their chance to be heroes and went home.

At some point during Charlie and Caril's stay at the Ward house, the letter addressed "for the law only" was composed. It gave the impression of being, in part, a written confession by Caril, admitting taking part in the murder of her family, and Chief Deputy Fahrnbruch questioned Charlie closely about it.

"Who wrote the letter?"

"I did."

"Who was present?"

"Caril."

"Did you figure out the language all by yourself?"

"What do you mean?"

"Did anybody tell you the things to put into that letter?"

"She was just talking, and I was writing it down. She was just saying it, and I was writing it down."

"You wrote down what she said?"

"Yes."

"Did you sign both of the names?"

"Yes. She wouldn't sign it, and got sore, so I signed it for both. It was in my jacket in Wyoming when we got picked up. Look, we didn't think we was going to be taken alive. That's why it was written. We had a few others, too. Notes."

"Why did you throw them out the window?"

"I said I was going to throw that one out. I thought I did, but I didn't. I don't know, we just threw them out the window."

"What did you write it for?"

"I just told you, we didn't think we'd be taken alive."

Caril denied taking any part whatever in writing the letter.

After Charlie had tied and gagged Mrs. Ward, he went downstairs and told Caril what had happened. According to Charlie, she said, "Well, don't tell the maid about it. She'll go ape shit."

Charlie asked her to watch the maid, and he went outside to move the cars. He pulled Mrs. Ward's Packard out of the garage, put Jensen's Ford in its place, and parked the Packard behind it so the Ford couldn't be so easily seen.

Back inside, he ransacked every closet and drawer, looking for guns and anything else he might like to have. He took some binoculars and brown gloves, neither of which he ever had a chance to use. He put on a white shirt and told Caril to pick out a different coat for herself. She put on what he termed a "westy-looking" jacket, made out of suede, and packed a suitcase full of clothes.

Around five-thirty, the city edition of the Lincoln *Journal* arrived with a picture, taken by Charlie's landlady, of him and Caril grinning into a camera. There was also a picture of Charlie's Ford stuck on the lane to Meyer's farm. Headlines read: FARMER FOUND YOUTHS SOUGHT. There were pictures of Caril's parents and her baby half sister. Smaller articles included a dated one concerning Carol King and Robert Jensen called COUPLE MISSING, and another called COLVERT CASE RECALLED.

They spent some time cutting pictures out of the paper, pictures which were later found in Caril's possession. They included snapshots of her slain family. The testimony she gave concerning the clippings, in answer to County Attorney Elmer Scheele's questioning in court, damaged her case:

"Now, Caril, while you were in the house there, did you look at any newspapers?"

"Yes. I didn't look at it. There was a newspaper there. The newspaper came, and he had it and cut out some pictures."

"And did you cut out any of the pictures?"

"Well, he cut part of them out and I cut the rest of them out."

"What pictures did you cut out?"

"The pictures of him and I."

"You cut that one out?"

"I helped cut that one out. He cut partway and I cut the rest."

"And is that picture — what kind of picture was that, Caril? Can you describe that?"

"It was Chuck and I sitting on a chair, and he had his cowboy boots on, and I had my regular shoes on."

"Did you cut out some other pictures, Caril?"

"I don't know whether he cut them out or I cut them out."

"What pictures were those?"

"Of my sister and mother and dad."

"And those pictures were in that paper also?"

"I think so."

"In any event, either you or he cut them out, is that right?"

"I think he cut them out."

"Were they in there when you cut out the picture of you and Chuck?"

"I don't know. I didn't get to see the paper. He wouldn't let me see it."

"You cut out the other picture, didn't you?"

"Yes."

"Were those, the pictures of your mother and dad and little sister, in the paper when you cut out the big picture?"

"No, they weren't in the paper. I didn't see them."

"Either you or he cut them out?"

"Yes."

"Do you know which one?"

"I think he cut them out, or I think I cut them out."

The testimony wasn't believed by the jury. It didn't seem credible to them that she could have had pictures of her family with her for almost twenty-four hours and not have seen them, or have realized their significance.

When they finished cutting the pictures out of the paper, Charlie told Caril to get his knife from the bedroom upstairs and wash it off, which she did. She later told Fahrnbruch that when she came back down she thought it smelled bad upstairs from Mrs. Ward's blood and that she had poured some perfume around. Mrs. Ward supposedly was tied and gagged on her bed, suffering from the wound Charlie had caused when he threw the knife in her back, but still alive. According to Charlie, she spent the day there after she had been wounded, and when he and Caril left the Ward's no further harm had been done to her. However, this was hardly the situation authorities would find later.

It was nearly 6:00 P.M., time for Lauer Ward to come home, and Charlie staked himself out with the .22 by the kitchen door. He had Caril watch for Ward through the dining room window, with orders to yell when he drove in the driveway. When Ward did pull in the drive in his Chevrolet, Caril called out and Charlie met the man at the kitchen door with the Ward's .22. According to Charlie, he told the man that nothing was wrong, that they were just going to tie him up and take his car. Ward said all right, but then grabbed the gun from Charlie and they began to fight over it. Charlie took the barrel of the gun and with it pushed Ward down the stairs into the basement. Charlie flipped the light switch at the top of the stairs and saw Ward lying on his back on the floor looking up. The gun, which had gone off when it hit the basement floor, was laying beside him. Charlie ran down the stairs and they began to fight for the gun again. Charlie got possession of it but Ward grabbed an electric iron and raised it over his head. "I just cocked the gun and pointed it at him," Charlie said later to Scheele, "and he put his hand back down . . . I told him that nothing was wrong and nothing was going to happen . . . he put the iron down on the floor."

But Ward then tried to run up the stairs and Charlie shot him in the back. Still, Ward kept going, through the kitchen and into the living room. He had the front door open when Charlie shot him again. Charlie said, "It probably struck him in the head . . . I was standing about five feet from him, maybe less . . . I asked him if he was all right and he didn't answer . . ."

In Charlie's formal statement to Elmer Scheele — one of his earlier confessions — he tried to maintain that Caril was innocent. However, there were discrepancies in the confession that made the investigators suspect his story. After Charlie killed Ward, Lillian Fencl ran down in the basement and hid. Caril told Charlie she thought the maid had a gun, so Charlie didn't go after her. Finally Lillian came up on her own, without a gun. Charlie said he took her upstairs and tied her up, told Caril to watch her, and started loading up canned goods for their trip west. He found some shoe polish, rubbed it in his hair to change the color, then called Caril down to rub it in the places he couldn't see. The following is Charlie's account to Scheele of what happened next.

"We left . . . I, I locked the front door and I turned off all the lights and I gave her the guns and told her to go on out and put them in the car."

Scheele asked, "And you got into Mrs. Ward's Packard, you and Caril?"

"Yes . . . I got ten dollars from the maid . . . I took about seven dollars from Mrs. Ward . . . upstairs in the bedroom laying on the table."

"Now did you at any time use your knife on Mrs. Ward after you threw it at her the first time?"

"No, she was alive when I left."

"Did you at any time use your knife on the maid?"

"Why, ain't the maid alive?"

"Did you ever touch Mr. Ward with your knife?"

"Well, was he stabbed? . . . No, I never touched him with the knife."

If Charlie's apparent gaps of knowledge are to be believed, he did not stab and kill Lillian Fencl, did not stab to death Mrs. Ward (though he did throw a knife in her back), did not inflict knife wounds on Lauer Ward. Yet all these things occurred. There was much speculation over what weapon was used on these victims, as well as the one used to mutilate the body of Carol King. The deep, narrow wounds appeared to have been made with a long, rigid blade, probably double-edged, such as a bayonet or stiletto. Charlie's hunting knife, which had a broad blade, would not have made the same type of wounds. The foot-long black-handled kitchen knife possibly could have made them, but Dr. E. D. Zeman, who performed the autopsies, doubts it. "Kitchen knives are generally flimsy," he says. "These wounds were made with a rigid blade, and probably one with a double cutting edge." A knife of this type was never found and neither was the kitchen knife. Charlie said they had, he thought, left a double-edged knife under a sofa cushion at the Bartletts', but police were unable to find it. He said he had had Caril throw the kitchen knife out the car window near Seward, Nebraska, after they had left the Ward's. Sherif Karnopp had a mounted posse search along the highway around Seward for both knives, but neither were found.

During this part of the interrogation, Charlie told Scheele

that he and Caril had argued a lot on the murder spree, not about what they were doing, but about their relationship. He said at one point he gave her his gun and told her to shoot him with it. Caril confirmed this to Fahrnbruch. She said she told him not to be silly and tossed the gun back to him.

But Caril's version of the day at the Ward hourse differed considerably from Charlie's, particularly concerning what happened to Mrs. Ward and Lillian Fencl. She told Fahrnbruch that when Charlie came downstairs after the encounter with Mrs. Ward, he said he had killed the woman — stabbed her in the throat with Velda Bartlett's kitchen knife. Caril said she washed off the knife for Charlie, then went upstairs and poured a large bottle of perfume on the rugs and on a chair outside Mrs. Ward's bedroom. She wouldn't admit to ever going in the bedroom. Later, she went back up to find a coat and had trouble deciding between a black one and the suede jacket she finally chose. She said that she drank a 7-Up while watching for Mr. Ward and, when he arrived, yelled, "He's coming in the driveway!" Then she hid in the downstairs bathroom. After Mr. Ward had been shot, they waited, both with loaded .22s, to see if anybody had heard the shots. When no one came to the house, they took the maid upstairs.

Fahrnbruch asked, "What did he do when you went upstairs, Caril?"

"He said for her to sit down in the chair, and I was looking out the window."

"What room were you in at that time?"

"One of the bedrooms."

"Was the light on?"

"No."

"Did you have anything in your hands other than the gun?"

"The light, the flashlight."

"And the maid was sitting in a chair in that bedroom?"

"Yes."

"Then what happened, Caril? You were looking out the window?"

"Well, he took a sheet and started tearing it, and then he started tying her wrists, and I told him why didn't he let her lay down on the bed because she would get tired from sitting up all night. I didn't know he was going to kill her then. And then he made her lay down on the bed and started tying her wrists."

"How did he tie her wrists?"

"With both hands together."

"So that the little fingers touched each other?"

"Yes, I think so. And then he tied them to the bedpost."

"Were her hands over her head or not?"

"Yes."

"Then what else did he do?"

"He tied her feet . . . To the end of the bed. She kept saying to turn on the light, she was scared of the dark."

"Did somebody turn on the light?"

"No."

"Did you hold the flashlight for him while he was tying her up?"

"I don't remember . . . I was looking out the window, and he started stabbing her, and she started screaming and hollering."

"Do you know what he stabbed her with?"

"My mother's knife."

"Did he say anything while he was stabbing her?"

"No, he put a pillow over her face."

"Did he stab her more than once . . . twice?"

"Yes . . . I heard it. Every time he stabbed her she moaned."

"About how many times did she moan?"

"More than five."

"Was she laying face-down on the bed or face-up?"

"Face-up."

"Now, she was laying that way when he tied her up? Did her hands continue to be tied to the top of the bed?"

"No, she broke them loose . . . When he was stabbing her."

"And what had he tied her to the top of the bed with?"

"A sheet."

"What about her feet, were they still tied to the bottom of the bed?"

"Yes."

"And then what happened after he had got done stabbing her?"

"He said he didn't think she was ever going to die. And then he said to shine the flashlight over there. And he cut the strips holding her legs and covered her over."

"What did he cover her up with?"

"A blanket that laid on the bed . . . I seen the blood on the bed, but I didn't see the stabs."

"You held the flashlight while he was cutting the legs from the bed?"

"Yes."

"Did you hold the light while he covered her up?"

"Yes. I held it on the floor."

"Where were you standing when he was doing that?"

"By the bed."

"Were you looking out the window, Caril?"

"Yes . . . To see if anybody was coming . . . He told me to shine the flashlight on his arm. There was blood stains all over his shirt, over the cuff of his shirt . . . He told me to find a clean shirt for him."

"What did you do?"

"I went and found a white shirt."

Earlier that day, about 5:30 P.M., Lauer Ward had had a conference with Nebraska's governor, Victor Anderson, in the governor's office. Anderson said later that they had looked at the newspaper articles about the recent murders, and when Lauer left he had been noticeably upset because of it. Ward went downtown after that to a liquor store, made a purchase, and chatted with the owner a few minutes before he went home. No one saw him arrive at the house, no one heard gunshots. The house immediately north of the Wards' was vacant at the time. During the evening no one stopped by the Wards'. Several people called but were not particularly bothered when no one answered. One person said a girl had answered the phone and said Mrs. Ward wasn't feeling well, but the caller thought nothing of it. Charlie said he had turned off the lights before he left, but neighbors reported seeing lights on in the house that night.

No one suspected anything was wrong until the next morning when Lauer didn't show up at the office. A cousin and business associate, Fred Ward, called the house and no one answered. He thought that someone should be there, and he called repeatedly throughout the morning without success. Shortly before noon he drove to the house and, after knocking, let himself inside.

Lauer Ward's body was just inside the front door, shot through the temple and back and stabbed in the neck. Mrs. Ward's body, dressed in her nightgown and wearing no underwear, was lying on the floor between two beds in one of the bedrooms. There was a knife wound in her back, but the cause of death was multiple stab wounds to her neck and chest. Lillian Fencl's body was found tied to a bed in another bedroom with multiple stab wounds to her chest and stomach and severe cuts on her hands, arms, and legs. Her mouth was open in a frozen scream. The Chesapeake, Queenie, was locked in the basement bathroom, and the poodle, Suzy, was cowering under a bed upstairs with a broken neck.

Because the condition of the bodies conflicted with Charlie's testimony, suspicion was aroused as to Caril's possible role in the murders. One impression was that Charlie was trying to cover up for her but had given himself away because he didn't know that Mrs. Ward and her housekeeper were dead. Later, he hinted that Caril might have killed Lillian Fencl, saying that after they had left the house he remembered her saying that the maid had tried to get away. "I don't know," he said. "Either she said the maid was trying to get away, and she didn't know whether to stab her or not. Maybe she did, I don't know." Later in his statement he quoted her as saying, "The maid wouldn't die" or "The maid didn't want to die."

Until now, the city of Lincoln had become increasingly alarmed with each series of murders, and Bennet felt as if it were under siege, but when news of the murders in the Ward household was released, Lincoln and the surrounding countryside verged on mass hysteria. Before, there was at least the chance that Charlie was out of the area, but now it appeared almost certain that he was still there and was going to continue killing until he was brought down. The death of the Wards and their maid showed that he would strike anywhere, seemingly at random, and the whole population felt vulnerable. Within seventy-two hours the public had been besieged with these and other banner headlines:

BELMONT FAMILY SLAIN
TOT AND PARENTS FOUND DEAD IN APPARENT MURDER

3 MORE BODIES FOUND
BENNET VICTIMS BRING TOLL TO 6

3 MORE BODIES FOUND TO BOOST
MURDERS TO 9; GUARD CALLED OUT

Many citizens no longer had faith in local law enforcement, and there was a rush to buy guns and ammunition. Don

Stokes, salesman in a local hardware store, said, "People bought anything that would shoot. They weren't particular. We had to make four or five trips to the warehouse. In just one two-hour period I'd estimate that we sold thirty-five to forty rifles and pistols." Most bought weapons to protect themselves and their families, but around 100 citizens, many intoxicated and hysterical, tried unsuccessfully to join a sheriff's posse forming at the courthouse. The attitude was: "Somebody's got to stop that maniac."

Immediately after the bodies at the Ward residence were found, Governor Anderson called out 200 members of the National Guard, and they were soon cruising the streets with jeeps armed with mounted machine guns. Parents with guns drawn rushed to the schools and took their children home. The city was completely sealed off. A block by block search began. The FBI started an investigation. A thousand-dollar reward was offered by the mayor. Aircraft were sent up to help look for the Ward's black Packard.

At one point, police radioed that they had spotted the Packard and were giving chase. They finally forced the fleeing car to stop and found the driver to be a prominent Lincoln attorney who was out having a little fun with the desperate situation.

Telephone lines to the police station were jammed with hundreds of calls reporting the car with the fleeing couple. Other calls flooded in from hysterical housewives who had milkmen, mailmen, bread men at the door. One Lincoln *Journal* reporter went home armed with large copy-desk shears. One woman almost shot her husband with a shotgun when he came home from work. A University of Nebraska student who resembled Charlie was forced to go into hiding.

Marilyn Coffey, a writer who lived in Lincoln at the time, said in a recent article in *The Atlantic Monthly*, "I still remember where I was when I heard that murderers Caril Ann

Fugate and Charles Starkweather were 'on the loose' in our town. It was one of those moments suspended permanently in time — like the day my father heard the news about Pearl Harbor on the car radio as he crossed a certain bridge south of town. Or the day FDR died. Or the day, a generation later, when I froze before a barroom TV set listening to details of a report that Kennedy had been shot."

The panic, on a lesser scale, spread over the state. Traveling in a fast car, Charlie and Caril could possibly be anywhere. They were reported sighted in various parts of Nebraska, Kansas, Iowa, Missouri, and Oklahoma.

The story was heralded in the papers as one of the worst multiple murders in United States history. Charlie was major news all over the country. Most of the coverage was responsible but some gave a *Detective Story* cast to the nightmare. This story was printed in the Omaha *World-Herald* while Charlie and Caril were still on the loose.

Fear Rouses Countryside
With Multiple Killer Abroad

Bennet, Neb. — Terror stalked the countryside Tuesday night. Farm houses became armed camps and grim-lipped men and women here, 16 miles southeast of Lincoln, burned lights far past the usual bedtime.

There was only one conversation topic — a gun-crazy teenage murder suspect and his 14-year-old girl friend.

Where would Charles R. Starkweather, 19, strike next?

Was his girl friend, Carol [sic] Fugate, a willing accessory, dead herself or accompanying the youth out of terror?

Authorities working around the clock said there is no doubt the stubby, green-eyed youth with a shock of red hair worn in a popular teen-age style is responsible for the six killings.

"All our deductions add up to the same answer," said Lincoln Police Chief Joe Carroll.

"Starkweather is our man. I just. hope he doesn't kill anyone else."

"Never in my 27 years on the force have I seen anything to compare with these wanton murders," Mr. Carroll declared.

"That goes for me, too," said Assistant Chief Eugene Masters. "There can't be any other answer."

Horror mounted in Lincoln and throughout Southeastern Nebraska as dusk fell and the word got around that three more killings had been added to the triple murder discovered in Lincoln Monday.

Volunteer posses were formed.

Off-duty policemen and other law enforcement officers called control points with offers to work around the clock on their time.

In farm houses shotguns, rifles and pistols were taken from closets and racks and placed in strategic, easy-to-reach places.

Mrs. Conrad Leader, who with her husband operates a filling station here, paused while sounding the 6 o'clock whistle.

"Three-quarters of the men in this town were on the hunt for Carol and Robert (Carol King, 16, and Robert Jensen, 17) all day," she said.

"My husband was among them. No one carried a gun. I'll guarantee you they will all be carrying guns when they go out again."

Herbert Randall, hardware store operator, appeared haggard after his all-day search. He looked at his powerful hands with hard eyes, started to say something and stopped. He walked out of the station.

On the porch of a modest home on a muddy street here, Warren King, 26-year-old brother of Carol, stood with jutted jaw, fighting back tears.

"When she left Monday night she told me she would have Bob bring her home at about 10:30," he said.

"I knew something was wrong when she didn't come home, but I didn't think it was going to end like this."

He said that Carol had been living with him and his wife because their father had died of a heart attack three weeks ago.

"And then came this . . . and then came this!"

Those who knew 70-year-old August Meyer, who was slain on

the back porch of his well-kept, white, two-story farm house, were outraged as well as grieved.

"Augie kept as nice a farm as you will find," said a friend.

"He cared for his mother until she died not too long ago. And then along comes this kill-crazy punk and shoots him."

As the night wore on the lights in the small town and farm houses continued to glow.

No women or children walked the streets.

Terror stalked the countryside.

The Reverend Peter Raible, in a sermon later delivered at the Lincoln Unitarian Church, gave a more considered account of what people were going through: "At the height of the Starkweather manhunt, all of us believed that a ruthless killer roamed our city. We had no idea where he was; we knew that our personal chances of meeting him were slight; but we also knew that he struck suddenly, apparently at random and without warning. Many housewives were home alone; families were divided among home, school and work. This isolation led to a growing panic. We were afraid and we were alone . . ."

Reverend Raible went on to say that, because no one who met Starkweather lived to tell the story, the police and news media had no authoritative word on what was happening — so the public believed the worst. The police, always several corpses behind Charlie and Caril, could no longer be counted on. False tips, weird and fantastic rumors added to the situation. People began to fly apart. Work and school ground to a halt. The panic and confusion spread.

Chapter SIX

WHEN CHARLIE AND CARIL left the Ward house in Lauer Ward's black 1956 Packard, they cruised around town and for an unexplained reason once again went by the Bartlett residence. There was a car in the driveway and a light on in the kitchen; they kept going. For the second time they headed west, this time on Highway 34. Their destination was still Washington State.

Outside Seward, Nebraska, Charlie said Caril crawled over into the back seat and changed shirts. The plaid shirt she had been wearing was the same one she had on in the picture in the paper that day. She threw the old shirt, along with a blue one belonging to Charlie, out the window. This is probably also where she threw out the kitchen knife. Charlie's cold was bothering him, and he was exhausted, but nevertheless was still sexually stimulated by the murders. About 10:00 P.M., about thirty minutes before reaching Grand Island, Nebraska, he asked Caril for sexual relations. According to Charlie, her response was the same as after Carol King had been murdered: "You've had yours for the day."

Fahrnbruch asked Charlie later, "Had you had it that day before with Caril?"

"No, I didn't have it that day with her."

"What did she mean, that you already had it that day?"

"Well, she probably thought I screwed old lady Ward."

"Well, did you?"

"Hell no."

Autopsy reports confirmed that Mrs. Ward had not been sexually attacked.

In Grand Island they pulled into a service station. The operator's wife, Mrs. Walter Cummings, came out and explained that her husband had left for a few minutes and that she didn't know how to operate the pumps. She returned to the station office and, five minutes later, saw that the Packard was still there. She went back out. "Do you still want gas?"

"Not now," Charlie said. "I may be back later." He drove away with Caril lying under a blanket in the front seat. They filled up at another station in town and got on Highway 2 which took them across the sparsely populated Sand Hills of Nebraska. Since the only trip Caril had ever made before had been to the Sand Hills, she could not say she had been anywhere new on this trip until they were through them. As the small towns passed, she checked off their names on the map. According to Charlie, they wrote notes telling what they had done and threw them out the window along the way. He also said he wrote a brief confession on a service station restroom wall somewhere while still in Nebraska. The notes and the message on the wall were never reported found.

In Broken Bow at about two in the morning, Charlie pulled into the Bow Oil Company, operated by Edward Bolen. Bolen and others hanging around the station, and at the adjoining café, noted the Lancaster County plates and thought Charlie acted odd. He bought gas, then asked for a map of Nebraska. When Bolen said he was out, Charlie asked for a map of every other state he had. Bolen gave him the maps and offered to help with directions, but Charlie said, "I guess it don't matter."

A few hours later, Charlie fell asleep at the wheel and plunged into a ditch, but he regained control and got back on the highway. The car was undamaged but Charlie stopped anyway, saying he had to rest. Caril wanted him to keep going. He told her he thought that if they made love it would wake him up enough to drive another hour at least. She finally gave in. Afterward, Charlie drove another five or ten minutes, then pulled off the road and went to sleep.

While they were parked, a Broken Bow truck driver, Maynard Behrends, on the way to Alliance, saw the apparently unoccupied car and wrote down the license number. Later, returning from Alliance after his delivery, he saw the Packard proceeding west and called in a description to the Nebraska Safety Patrol. He thought it was unusual for somebody so young to have that nice a car. Behrends was later credited with being the first to spot Starkweather, but the patrol didn't broadcast the report until the victims at the Wards' home were discovered hours later. By that time Charlie and Caril were out of the state.

They proceeded past Ellsworth, then Charlie realized he needed more gas and returned to the town rather than take a chance on running out. The operator of the station where they stopped, Roy Graham, thought Charlie acted jumpy and, on a hunch, he later notified the Safety Patrol. That tip, too, was broadcast but did not lead to the capture.

After filling up, they continued on through Alliance, took another half-hour nap, then stopped for gas at Crawford, at the intersection of Highway 2 and Highway 20. People there thought Charlie's straw hat — which had belonged to August Meyer — looked out of season. He and Caril bought a full tank of gas, some candy bars for breakfast, nine bottles of Pepsi-Cola, then turned onto Highway 20. Fifteen minutes later, at about 9:00 A.M., they crossed the state line into Wyoming.

The name "Wyoming" comes from a combination of Delaware Indian words meaning either "Great Plains" or "End of the Plains" and the sixty-six miles from the state line to the town of Douglas is a broad expanse of wind-swept grazing land about 5000 feet above sea level. The atmosphere is clear and the Blue Mountain regions to the west and south seem to loom closer than they actually are. The area southwest of Douglas is typical badlands country, with deep gashes cutting through the plains, draining it dry within hours after a heavy rain. The old-style cowboys Charlie loved so much once roamed the area, and tribes like the Crow Nation, Arapaho, Shoshone, and Cheyenne hunted and made war here before the great Indian massacres of the 1880s.

Once out of Nebraska, chances of actually getting away seemed somewhat better, and they began to take their time, frequently stopping to rest. It took three hours for them to make the one-hour drive from the state line to Douglas. But as they neared the small town, they heard over the radio that the bodies at the Wards' had been found and that the murder suspects might be traveling in a 1956 Packard. In Douglas, Charlie became certain he was recognized. Everyone looked at them as they drove the conspicuous car with the Nebraska plates down the broad main street. Charlie hurried on through. By the time he was on Highway 87 toward Casper, he had decided to get another car at the first possible moment. Ten miles west of Douglas they saw one parked on the side of the highway. They stopped but the car was locked and there were no keys inside; they drove on.

After another mile and a half, near the Ayers Park and Natural Bridge turn off, they saw a Buick off the highway on a little road by a borrow pit, where the land had been excavated and used elsewhere as fill. Charlie parked beside the highway, about a hundred feet from the car, and walked over to it. There was a thirty-seven-year-old man, a traveling shoe salesman from Montana named Merle Collison, asleep in the front seat. The door was locked. Charlie tapped on the window on the driver's side until Collison woke up. According to Charlie, he said to the man, "Unlock your door."

Collison asked what for.

"We're going to trade cars."

Collison refused and Charlie walked back across the highway to the Packard. He returned with his .22 pump, put it up to the glass, and began firing. An autopsy later revealed that the salesman was shot once in the nose, once in the cheek, once in the neck, twice in the chest, once in the left arm, once in the right wrist, and twice in the left leg. But there were only two shots fired through the window. Charlie's stories about the death of Collison conflict. According to Reinhardt, this was one murder which worried him later. It was so cold-blooded that there was no way even he could rationalize self-defense; he thought people would think him cowardly because of the way the salesman died. Finally he settled on the story that Caril killed him. "I shot him," he said later, "but Caril finished him off." He claimed in a letter to County Attorney Elmer Scheele that after shooting the man twice through the window his gun jammed, and he called for Caril to bring another gun over. Collison, he wrote, agreed after he had been shot to let them have the car, but when he got out he started to struggle. "Caril was standing behind the car . . . he had a lot of fight left in him . . . Caril began shooting at him . . . while she was shooting he said something about a wife and kids . . . Caril said that was too bad and was calling him a lot of names."

123

After Collison was dead — the body slumped across the front seat and down on the floorboard on the passenger's side — Caril got in the back seat and Charlie started the car. But he couldn't release the hand brake. According to Caril, he turned to the body of Collison and said hopefully, "Man? Man? Are you dead?" But the body would not help him.

Moments later, a twenty-nine-year-old geologist, Joe Sprinkle from Casper, drove by. He later told reporters what happened: "I was traveling east toward Douglas when I passed a 1956 Packard on the side of the road. A new model Buick was facing west on the opposite side of the road. As I passed I did not see anyone in the vehicles, but I looked in my rearview mirror and saw someone get out of the Packard. I thought they had had an accident, so I turned my car around and came back. I pulled in behind the Buick and I saw Starkweather open the car door. Then I asked, 'Can I help you?' He straightened up with a rifle he had behind him and said, 'Raise your hands. Help me release the emergency brake or I'll kill you.' It was then I noticed the dead man behind the wheel. As I approached him, I grabbed at the gun and we fought for it in the middle of the highway. I knew that if he won I would be dead, so I managed to wrestle it from him."

While Sprinkle and Charlie were fighting, a Wyoming deputy sheriff named William Romer happened along in his patrol car and saw the struggle. He stopped about seventy feet away. Suddenly Caril sprang out of the back seat of the Buick and ran down the road to Romer's car. According to Romer, she got in and said, "Take me to the police."

Romer said, "Well, I'm a deputy sheriff."

Sobbing, Caril said, "He's killed a man!"

"Where?"

She pointed. "There."

"Who is he?"

She couldn't get his name out at first, then said, "Charles Starkweather."

Meanwhile Charlie was making his escape. Romer said in court, "Mr. Starkweather looked up and seen my car. They both had their hands on the gun. He just whirled and let go of the gun and Sprinkle went over into the borrow pit." Charlie ran across the highway to the Packard and drove off, headed back toward Douglas. Romer watched to make sure he wasn't going to double back, radioed Douglas for a roadblock, and started off in pursuit.

The call was received by Douglas Chief of Police Robert Ainslie, who was accompanied in his patrol car by Earl Heflin, sheriff of Converse County, Wyoming. Ainslie, short and be-spectacled, and Heflin, tall and wearing a ten-gallon hat, looked as if they might have been the inspiration for *"The Andy Grif-fith Show."* Nothing much happened around Douglas in the fifties — the Old West shootouts were far in the past — and Heflin was the first to admit he rarely fired his weapons and "couldn't hit the broad side of a barn." He and Ainslie had been following the events in Nebraska with interest, and they were grateful that Lincoln was so far away. Now, here was Starkweather himself — with nobody between him and the town except the two of them. They met Charlie about five miles outside of Douglas. They weren't sure it was he because Sheriff Romer had told them the wrong make of car. But as the Packard flew by, the person behind the wheel looked like Stark-weather, so they turned around and gave chase. Charlie had a good lead and hurtled into Douglas at over 100 miles an hour. But then he got caught in the traffic on the main drag and the police car caught up with him. The police car's siren and red lights were on, and when Heflin began firing at the Packard's tires with a .38 revolver everybody on the street scattered or hit the ground. Charlie passed a car on the right, then went left around a truck which was stopped at the red light in the middle of town. Ainslie was close on his tail and rammed the left rear of the Packard, locking bumpers, but the Packard's bumper ripped loose. A moment later Charlie was back on the open highway, headed for Nebraska. Both of the high-powered cars were going flat-out — "120 mph — or faster!" Ainslie claimed later. Now that they were out of town, Heflin, leaning out the window, was able to use his .30/30 carbine. After firing several shots, he hit the back window of the Packard, shattering the safety glass so that it was impossible to see inside the car. The Packard continued for a few seconds, disappearing in a dip in the road for a moment, and when it reappeared the brake lights were on. Charlie came to a dead stop in the middle of the highway.

Ainslie and Heflin parked a hundred yards behind the car and waited until Charlie got out. They yelled at him to put up his hands and, when he didn't, Ainslie shot at the ground at Charlie's feet and told him to lie down. Charlie reached, it appeared, for something in his back pocket and Ainslie fired again. But Charlie wasn't reaching for anything in his pocket: he was tucking in his shirttail. By the third time Ainslie fired, Charlie had his shirt the way he wanted it and he lay face-down on the highway. The officers approached cautiously and handcuffed him. Charlie was bleeding badly from the ear, and he thought he had been shot, but actually he had been cut by a flying piece of glass. Heflin said later, "He wouldn't say anything till we got him in the car. I had him handcuffed with his hands behind him, and when I straightened him up in the seat he said the handcuffs was a-hurtin' him, and if I didn't loosen them up he wouldn't tell me anything." Heflin made him more comfortable and asked Charlie why he had stopped so suddenly, right in the middle of the road. Charlie shrugged and said, "I would've hit head on with somebody, anyhow." Heflin said to reporters later that Charlie was meek once he was in the patrol car, then added, "He thought he was bleeding to death. That's why he stopped. That's the kind of yellow sonofabitch he is."

On the drive to the Douglas jail, Charlie said only one other thing: "Don't be rough on the girl. She didn't have a thing to do with it."

Caril, who was still in Deputy Sheriff Romer's car as he futilely tried to catch up with Charlie, had been saying the same thing. Romer later told reporters: "She told me she had always been a hostage but did not say one way or another that she tried to get away from Starkweather. She said that her home in Lincoln had been the headquarters for a group of two or three teen-agers with Starkweather who planned to rob a Lincoln bank. She had been held captive in the Bartlett home and they had left only when the other teen-agers chickened out on the bank robbery plan." Then Caril made the statement that would destroy her case in court. Romer said, "She told me she had seen all nine murders in Nebraska." If this is true, she could hardly have stayed with Charlie out of fear for her family's safety, which was the basis of her story. After that, Romer said, Caril ". . . finally wound down and became unintelligible. I couldn't tell for sure what she was saying sometimes. Her memory seemed to get progressively worse as we got her near the jail."

The two were put in the Converse County jail, which also contained the apartment home of Sheriff Heflin. Charlie was locked in a cell on the ground floor and Caril, who was taken care of by Heflin's wife, Hazel, was locked in a cell for women upstairs. Caril seemed to go into shock and would speak to no one. Hazel Heflin later spoke of the girl's condition: "She had been crying and her face was dirty, and you could see where the tears had run down her face, and her hair was a mess and her clothes were dirty, and she hadn't had a bath. She needed a bath pretty bad. She smelled." Caril refused all efforts to clean her up. She wouldn't take off her clothes. A doctor who came to give her a medical examination left in frustration; she wouldn't let him close to her. She was put under sedation and slept during much of her stay in Wyoming.

Charlie was filthy when he was brought in, his shirt was torn and splattered with blood from his ear, and his hair was covered with shoe polish. But he was not difficult about bathing; he just wasn't given the opportunity. He would not talk to reporters, or to the Wyoming law officers, except to say to Heflin and Ainslie, "You wouldn't have caught me if I hadn't stopped. If I'd had a gun I would have shot you." The only weapons he had had during the chase were his hunting knife and the empty .32 pistol.

Charlie complained about his ear hurting and about some glass in his hand, and as Douglas began to be besieged with reporters and photographers from over the nation, he became even more withdrawn. He was eventually left alone with pencil and paper, and he quickly wrote his family.

Dear Mon and Dad. i'm a way i hate to write this or maybe will not read it, but if you will i would like to have you read it, it would help me a lot.

i'm sorry for what i did in a lot of ways cause i know i hurt everybody, and you and mon did all you could to rise me up right and you all ways help me when i got in bad with something But this time i would like you not to do any thing to help me out. i hope you will under stand. . . . it would make me happy if everbody well go on just like anything didn't happen. the cops up here have been more than nice to me but these *dam* reporters, the next one that comes in here he is going to get a glass of water.

But dad i'm not real sorry for what i did cause for the first time me and Caril have more fun, she help me a lot, but if she comes back don't hate her she had *not* a thing to do with the Killing all we wanted to do is get out of town.

tell every body to take care. Chuck

Lincoln received word of the capture less than three hours after the bodies had been found at the Ward residence, thus avoiding possible further calamity caused by panicked citizens. Today, Sheriff Merle Karnopp says, "I hate to think what might have happened after dark that Wednesday if they hadn't been captured. People would have been shooting at anything that moved. There were a lot of armed men who had been drinking who were roaming around town."

Two Kansas City *Star* reporters with a private plane were in Lincoln covering the story, and Lincoln Police Lieutenant Robert Henninger caught a ride with them to Douglas, arriving around 9:30 P.M. the same day. Today, Henninger, retired from the force and a seller of "antiques and collectables," thumbs through his notes on the case. "I arrived in Douglas with thirty-five cents in my pocket and no toothbrush. Of course, I went to the jail immediately. It was swarming with reporters, and phone calls were coming in from all over the world. Well, Sheriff Heflin was busy with all this. He said I couldn't see Charlie — he was his prisoner and nobody else was getting in to see him. He gave me a hell of a time. I finally told him, 'Look, we don't know how many more people he shot in Nebraska who might still be alive. We need to find out so we can get to them.' "

Heflin then took Henninger to Charlie's cell, said, "There's the yellow sonofabitch," and left them to talk. Charlie seemed glad to see someone from home, and Henninger, an experienced interrogator, soon had him talking. Within hours Charlie was writing out a confession. He wrote that he killed Caril's parents before she came home from school. He admitted killing everyone on the murder trail except Clara Ward and Lillian Fencl. He said when he left the Wards', "There was only one dead person in that house."

The next morning banner headlines around the country announced the capture. One of the more startling appeared in the Omaha *World-Herald*:

PUNK'S BLOOD-STAINED STRING ENDS
AT 10 DEAD WITH WYOMING CAPTURE

On that morning, Charlie was formally charged by Sheriff Heflin for the murder of Merle Collison. Under other circumstances he would have been kept in Wyoming and tried for this crime. However, Wyoming's governor, Milward Simpson, was opposed to capital punishment and had already made a statement to the effect that, no matter what Charlie had done, he would commute a death sentence to life imprisonment. But he also said that, in view of the fact that at least nine people had been murdered in Nebraska, he was not opposed to turning jurisdiction over to the neighboring state. Nebraska's Governor Anderson, it was known, was not opposed to the death penalty. Simpson said that, if asked by Anderson, he would sign extradition papers "in a jiffy." He was asked, immediately.

Six Nebraska city and county officials, including Lancaster County Attorney Elmer Scheele and Sheriff Merle Karnopp, flew to Douglas late Thursday in an Air National Guard C–47 to bring Charlie and Caril back to Nebraska. As soon as they arrived at Sheriff Heflin's office, Charlie asked to see his "buddy," Sheriff Karnopp. Charlie had once lived across from the old Lancaster County jail where the Karnopp family had lived for eighteen years, and he had gone to school with the sheriff's son, Dennis. Karnopp walked down the gray corridor to the cell and Charlie, obviously glad to see him, grinned and said, "How's Dennis?"

Charlie talked willingly to the Nebraska authorities, explaining that he had wanted to be an outlaw ever since he was a child, but not this big a one. He said that hatred had just built up inside of him and that what he had done was a way for him to "be somebody." He wanted to know what else he could have done, anyway, with all those people coming at him like they had.

Elmer Scheele introduced himself to Charlie and said he was going to do everything he could to send him to the electric chair. Charlie seemed to enjoy the remark. There was no problem getting either Charlie or Caril to sign extradition waivers which would enable them to be immediately returned to Nebraska. Scheele said that the papers were fully explained to the couple and that "they knew what they were doing." But Caril said later that she had no idea what she was signing. And Charlie did not know about the Wyoming governor's views on capital punishment. Wyoming had a gas chamber which hadn't been used in over two decades, whereas Nebraska used an electric chair. Charlie's purported reason for signing: "Wyoming uses the gas chamber, and I don't like the smell of gas."

Once the papers had been signed, Scheele decided to begin the trip to Lincoln by motor caravan that same evening. Neither Charlie or Caril wanted to fly, and Charlie might have refused to sign the extradition papers if he couldn't travel by car. To save time, Scheele agreed. Also, an auto trip would give the opportunity for extensive questioning. The fact that Charlie was thought to be afraid to fly was a source of humor at the time, but Sheriff Karnopp says the idea was ridiculous. "Charlie wasn't afraid of anything of that nature. He was a daredevil. He wanted to put off being put in prison as long as possible so that he might have more time and opportunity to escape. He was always looking for a chance to get away." Karnopp goes on to say that once when Charlie was in his office in handcuffs, he told Karnopp he had to go to the bathroom. Karnopp said, "Sure, go ahead."

"Well, take off the handcuffs."

"You know I can't do that, Charlie."

"Why, I'll pee in my pants."

"I can't help that."

"All right, then, I just won't go."

The caravan which was to take them back consisted of four cars, with Charlie and Caril to travel separately in the two center ones. Caril was not required to wear handcuffs but Charlie was outfitted with leg shackles, handcuffs, and a leather transportation belt with a chain on it by which he could be led. When the two were taken out of the Douglas jail to be put in the cars, there was a great crowd of citizens gathered in the streets, along with about thirty photographers and writers from various national magazines and papers. Hazel Heflin, the sheriff's wife, was to ride in the car with Caril as far as Gering, Nebraska, where the travelers would spend the night.

The trip to Gering, made at night, was uneventful. But a mob of photographers and reporters were waiting when they arrived at the Gering jail. They wanted to know what Charlie had said on the way. By this time, he had admitted to Karnopp the killing of Robert Colvert which, when released to reporters, caused a storm of criticism to be directed at Lincoln law enforcement. The unavoidable conclusion: if that murder had been solved, ten people now dead would still be alive.

The next morning Charlie, standing on the commode in his cell in Gering, wrote another confession high up on a wall where it would not be easily noticed. With a pencil borrowed from a trustee, he made these statements:

> Caril is the one who said to go to Washington state.
> by the time any body will read this i will be dead for all the killings *then they cannot give caril the chair to.*
> from Lincoln Nebraska they got us Jan 29, 1958.
> 1958 Kill 11 persons
> Charles kill 9) all men
> Caril kill <u>2)</u> all girls
>   11

They have so many cops and people watching us leave i can't add all of them of.

There was also a heart drawn on the wall with an arrow through it. Inside the heart was written: "Charles Starkweather and Caril Fugate."

Because six males and five females had in fact died the defense argued in court that Charlie's figures indicated a diseased mind. Sheriff Karnopp, however, said that Charles had later explained to him why the numbers were wrong. Karnopp was walking to the cell just as Charlie was writing the figures, and Charlie was afraid of being caught. He knew eleven people had died so he just put down two figures which totaled eleven. It was all he had time to do.

Mrs. Karnopp joined the caravan in Gering. She got in the car with Caril, enabling Mrs. Heflin to return to Douglas. Mrs. Heflin, who had been the only one to talk to Caril at length since the capture, said to newsmen, "I don't think she knows her mother is dead." That was the first indication that Caril's story was changing.

When Gertrude Karnopp sat down in the car beside her, Caril said, "Are my folks dead?" Mrs. Karnopp looked at her without answering and Caril said, "Who killed them?"

"Don't you know, Caril?"

She said that the first she had heard of it was from Mrs. Warick, the wife of the sheriff in Gering. According to Mrs. Karnopp, Caril was talkative for a while, describing the death of August Meyer, catching the ride with the Bennet teen-agers, the day at the Wards, and how the maid seemed as if she would never die. She remarked that most of Mrs. Ward's clothes were too big for her but that the blouse and suede jacket she had on had belonged to the woman. She rubbed the sleeve of the coat, which had blood on it, and said, "Isn't this the prettiest jacket, though?" She talked about her family, saying that her stepfather was too strict and that she hadn't liked him very well. She showed Mrs. Karnopp the pictures of her family which had been clipped out of the paper at the Wards'. She talked about her sister Barbara and about a telegram Barbara had sent to Douglas, pledging moral support. Caril said ruefully, "But you just wait. She won't have a thing to do with me when we get back." Then she said that the papers had written that the three bodies had been shot where they were found, but really they had been shot in the house and carried out.

Mrs. Karnopp stared at her. "Which bodies do you mean, Caril?"

Caril didn't answer immediately, then said, "Mr. Meyer was shot in the house and then drug outside." After that she refused to talk at all and occupied herself by making little dolls out of Kleenex.

Today Mrs. Karnopp dispels the myth that Caril was pregnant during this time. The story, popular even today, is that Caril had the baby in secret in prison and it was adopted by her sister Barbara. Mrs. Karnopp says, "I was with her every moment on the trip to Lincoln, and I know she couldn't have been pregnant because she was having her period."

Crowds were gathered along the road at the different towns on the way back. "It was like a parade," Sheriff Karnopp said. Charlie ignored the people but Caril was pleasant to them, waving and smiling. Once she tried to roll down her window to talk, but Mrs. Karnopp stopped her.

She wasn't friendly with Charlie, however. In fact, she seemed to get more and more angry with him as the trip neared its end. At a stop in North Platte, she glared at him every time they were in sight of each other, and once she held up one of her Kleenex dolls where he could see it and wrung its neck.

In an effort to avoid the crowds along the way, they got gas at state government facilities, and instead of going to a restaurant they had a picnic lunch in an open area near Kearney.

For security reasons, Charlie was to be taken directly to the Nebraska State Penitentiary rather than the city or county jail.

He would be put in a cell in the prison hospital. Caril would then be taken on to the state hospital and kept there. They arrived at the west gate of the prison around 6:30 P.M. and were greeted by another crowd of newsmen, photographers, and movie cameramen. Caril, her head covered by a scarf, smiled tightly into the lenses. Charlie pretended to ignore the attention, but nevertheless was the better subject. Bloodied, in chains, shaggy-haired, a cigarette dangling from his lips, wearing his black leather motorcycle jacket, tight black denim pants, blue and white cowboy boots with a butterfly design on the toes — he was a perfect-looking young rebel-killer. But it was a fleeting image which he projected for the last time. From now on his appearance, as well as everything else to do with the closing days of his life, was in the hands of his keepers.

Chapter SEVEN

THE SEVENTEEN MONTHS Charlie spent in the Nebraska State Penitentiary were as transitional for the country outside as they were for him. Within days of his incarceration, the United States managed to get an *Explorer* satellite to stay in orbit. Elvis the Pelvis became Private Presley — redeeming himself in the eyes of parents all over the country by permitting his sideburns to be clipped, but losing status with his younger followers. It was upsetting to the precarious teen-age culture, which was still mourning the 1955 death of James Dean, but an even harder blow — marking the end of the decade and perhaps of a way of life — came in the winter of 1959 when a plane crash took the lives of the enormously popular rock-and-roll singers Buddy Holly, J. P. Richardson ("the Big Bopper"), and Ritchie Valens.

For Charlie it was a period of introspection, at least token atonement, sincere, if limited, artistic endeavor, and perhaps an opportunity to enjoy his infamy. His life had by now taken on such significance for him that he tried to express his feelings to the world by writing his own story. According to Reinhardt, he had no doubt but that it would be read by everybody and make his family rich.

When he arrived at the prison, he was bathed, shorn, deloused, outfitted in prison clothes, and given his private cell. He was the most heavily guarded prisoner in the history of the prison. Almost immediately, mail for Charlie started arriving, but it was censored and he never saw most of it. People he had never met came to see him but were turned away by the deputy warden, John Greenholtz. Charlie had little time to himself — he was continually being interrogated, examined physically and mentally, and prepared for his days in court.

Public reaction to the case was enormous. Teen-age crime and violence were on the rise, and people wondered if Charlie's murder spree might be the beginning of a trend. The possibility was upsetting enough to be made the subject of numerous editorials and letters to the press.

One editorial, published in Nebraska's Omaha *World-Herald* several days after the capture, said in part: "If Charles Starkweather were a case apart, a biological accident, a monstrous freak of nature, then today all Americans could take a deep breath of relief and give thanks that his mad career of murder had been brought to an end. But although his crimes were of a violence beyond precedent, nevertheless there was a certain flavor to the Starkweather story which brought back to mind a thousand others which have been told in recent years to an unbelieving America. The sideburns, the tight blue jeans, the black leather jacket — those have become almost the uniform of juvenile hoodlums. And the snarling contempt for discipline, the blazing hate for restraint, have become a familiar refrain in police stations and juvenile courts throughout the land. To a greater degree than ever before, influences are pulling some youngsters away from the orbit of the home, the school, and the church, and into the asphalt jungle. That is the problem. . . ."

Charlie and Caril were both charged with first degree murder in connection with the death of seventeen-year-old Robert Jensen: murder on the first count — with premeditation — and murder on a second count — in the perpetration of a robbery. Under Nebraska law, which allows for juveniles to be tried as adults for severe crimes, they both could be sent to the electric chair if found guilty. With ten Nebraska victims to choose from, the decision to try them for the murder of Robert Jensen was made by a process of elimination. The prosecution elected to select the murder which would most effectively shock the conscience of the judge and jury, and the death of Robert Jensen seemed the logical choice. Unlike the others, he was not a member of the families of the accused, he was not rich, he was not poor, he was not old, he was not the victim of an abnormal sexual attack — he was a clean-cut all-American boy, the opposite of Charlie Starkweather. Also, from statements taken from Charlie and Caril, it was indicated that Caril actively helped rob Jensen — held a gun on him and took his money. With some of the other murders, a case might be made that she was an innocent bystander, but with this one it didn't seem likely.

Both Charlie and Caril entered pleas of not guilty.

Since they could not afford to pay attorney fees, their attorneys had to be court-appointed and paid for by the state. A forty-seven-year-old Lincoln lawyer, John McArthur, was selected to defend Caril, and two other local lawyers, T. Clement Gaughan, fifty-four, and William F. Matschullat, fifty-two, were chosen to defend Charlie. The state appointed two lawyers for Charlie's defense because of the complexity of the case and its desire for a speedy trial.

When Judge Harry A. Spencer asked the two older, respected lawyers to defend Charlie, he told them, "The whole world is going to be watching this trial, and I want to appoint someone who will see that justice is served."

Clem Gaughan accepted the case with some reluctance. Because of Charlie's obvious guilt, Gaughan viewed the challenge as one of making sure that Charlie's constitutional rights were protected. "I'll do what I can," he told reporters. "But I can't pull rabbits out of a hat." The two lawyers divided their duties: Matschullat would be primarily responsible for research and preparing court briefs; Gaughan would present the case to the court. Charlie had pled not guilty, claiming self-defense, and though he was in earnest, the plea struck most people as ridiculous. His lawyers thought Charlie's only hope was probably an insanity plea, and they set about finding people qualified to determine if he was mentally ill. It was difficult. Most local psychiatrists whom they approached refused to testify if they couldn't appear in court as impartial witnesses. Finally, a Lincoln psychiatrist, John Steinman, reluctantly agreed because of the importance to society of having psychiatric tests made. A psychiatrist and a psychologist from Kansas City were also obtained.

The lawyers and the doctors met with considerable obstruction from Charlie, who was completely opposed to an insanity plea. The doctors proceeded with their tests as well as they could. Just as Charlie would not consent to a polygraph test by the police department, he would not allow the doctors to administer an electroencephalograph to test for brain damage. And because Charlie had a perforated eardrum — indicating a one-time infection near the brain — brain damage was at least a possibility.

When the doctors were done, they were unanimous in their view that Charlie was suffering from a diseased mind. His lawyers built their defense around their findings. Gaughan announced, "The plea will be changed to not guilty by reason of insanity — whether Charlie is for it or not."

From then on, Gaughan and Matschullat got little cooperation from Charlie or his family. Strangely, Charlie began instead to cooperate with the prosecution. Both he and his family seemed to prefer he die in the electric chair than be judged insane. As Charlie told Reinhardt: "Nobody remembers a crazy man."

As the trial, set for early May, approached, Charlie began to implicate Caril more and more deeply in the murders. At first he stuck with the story that she was his innocent hostage, but even on the trip back to Nebraska he had suggested that she could have gotten away if she had wanted. The scrawls on the jail-cell wall in Gering implicated her, but he claimed he thought no one would see what he wrote until it was too late. He had done it merely in the interest of history. And, in fact, no one did see the writing until Charlie told the authorities about it. Finally, in a letter to his prosecutor he accused Caril of killing Carol King:

> Charles Starkweather
> Box 111 Lincoln, Nebraska
> March 28, 1958

Dear Mr. Scheele:

i'n writing this at ny own free will and well sign it when done. It would take to nuch paper to tell why i change ny mind of what happen in Caril f part of Killing of Carol King? i Know my folks can tell you why i'n writing this. When i Kill the boy out at the cave by the school house, he drop on the steps and landed on the foor in the cave. the King girl never ran or said anything i told her to stay right where she was i gone on dowm into the cave and he was moving a little, show i got up out of the cave and Carol King was standing right where i left here. "i think she was Shock" i went to the car to get a flash light Caril fugate was siting in the front and with the 4.10, i gone down into the cave and was dowm there about 15 to 25 min. then i got scared and ran out of the cave and told King to go on down into the cave, and not even stay intull she got down she was on about the 2'd step and ran to the car, i was so dan scared i back of into a dichd. we got out of car to see what happen, i and caril went on back up to the cave and i told carol King to come on up. i gave the 22 cal. to caril fugate and told her to watch her, gone on back down to the car and was on the side jacking the car body up, then i heard a shot and ran back to the cave, caril said that King started to run and had to shot her. caril went on to car and got in it. i put the King girl in the cave, on about the 2 or 3 step from the top. the rest is in the statemind i gave you. when we got the car out i and caril walk up to the cave and past the door and some boards on the opening of the cave, if there is any details you would like to Know about the King case come out or asked ny folks to asked ne, and i'll tell you. and the nan that got Kill in wyoing, caril and i both shot hin! My writing is a little of a mess, but i hope you can read it.

Then, on April 9, he wrote another letter to Scheele — possibly in answer to a request for more detail — which was later made public. It said basically the same thing as the first letter but also gave his reason for writing it: "I'll be convicted for what I did and that's okay. But I'll be damned it I'll be sentenced for what I didn't do." He ended the letter by saying that Caril was the most trigger-happy person he had ever seen.

Caril's lawyer, John McArthur, viewed these accusations as absurd and proceeded to build his case around the "innocent hostage" theory. Caril would not go to trial until late October.

On April 24, Robert Colvert's nineteen-year-old widow, Charlotte, gave birth to a girl.

The trial, *State of Nebraska* v. *Charles Raymond Starkweather*, started on May 5 and lasted eighteen days. On the Monday morning it began, a gang of from ten to fifteen Bennet teen-agers who had vowed to kill Charlie gathered on the courthouse lawn and awaited his arrival. In boots, jeans, and T-shirts with the sleeves rolled up to the shoulder, the boys were dressed for action, but if they were armed they kept their weapons concealed. The gang was more loud than determined and, since it had been announcing its intentions for days, it was a simple matter for Sheriff Karnopp to send over a detachment of deputies to disperse the boys. The gang, however, was only one threat to Charlie's life, and the security force protecting the prisoner during the trip from prison to courthouse was one of the largest in Nebraska history. Besides the many uniformed officers from the police and sheriff's departments, there were armed plainclothes men all along the route — a number of them stationed on rooftops with high-powered rifles.

It was a balmy day outside, but the courtroom in the old county courthouse was stuffy — the windows having been closed for security reasons. As the slow process of jury selection got underway, the only thing interesting was Charlie himself. He looked respectable in the light tan suit provided by the penitentiary. He had gained fifteen pounds in prison, and despite his protests his hair was neatly trimmed. He wore a regular four-in-hand tie instead of the string tie he had requested and regular black shoes instead of the cowboy boots he wanted. At one point he playfully tugged at the long chain on his wrist which connected him to Sheriff Karnopp. He laughed and began swinging the heavy chain as if it were a jump rope. No one was amused.

Charlie was a reflection of the style of the fifties; his walk, his gestures, the slight tilt of his head were all just right — a perfect imitation of his Hollywood guides. On one strip of TV film taken during the trial, he emerged from the courthouse looking at first glance as though he might have been a young business-man. But his style still somehow showed through the exterior changes. He had a cigarette between his lips at just the right angle, and he paused at the top of the courthouse steps to take one last draw and to survey the crowd gathered below. His look was one of bored detachment. With flawless timing, he reached up with manacled hands for his cigarette, flicked it to the concrete and stepped on it. Then, flanked by armed guards, he proceeded quickly to the waiting car. His legs didn't seem nearly so bowed as he had written that they were, and he moved with the easy, rolling grace of a boxer or wrestler. Except for the handcuffs he might have been a rock-and-roll star or a visiting dignitary coping with the familiar hassle of crowds. All of his life, he had dreamed of such fame, and now he acted like it had been his all along.

It took four days to select a jury and three days for the prosecution to present its case. To get a first-degree murder conviction, County Attorney Scheele had to prove that a murder was committed, that the accused did it, that he did it with premeditation or while committing a felony, and that he was sane. All except the last element was a relatively simple matter and was accomplished by obtaining testimony from the victim's father, the pathologist who performed the autopsy, and various other witnesses. Then photos were introduced and portions of Charlie's statements, in which he admitted the crime, were read. It was not necessary to prove Charlie sane until the defense presented evidence to the contrary, and on May 13 the state rested its case.

The job facing the defense was considerably more difficult. The definition of legal sanity, as contained in the McNaghten formula, does not always have a great deal to do with actual or medical insanity — it is quite possible to be medically insane yet be decalred sane in court. Stated simply, the McNaghten formula, created in 1843 in England by the House of Lords, asks these questions: Did the accused know the nature and quality of the act or the acts with which he is charged? Did he know the act with which he is charged was wrong when he did it?

Obviously, a knowledge of right and wrong does not guarantee the ability to adhere to that knowledge. A person may be completely mad and still know the difference between the two — he may just be out of control to the point he is unable to act on the knowledge. Nevertheless, irresistible impulse is not considered grounds for insanity in most of the United States. The only real hope of a defense attorney to get an insanity verdict — except in cases where the murderer has no awareness of reality and obviously demonstrates it — is to convince the jury by overwhelming evidence that the individual should be considered insane, regardless of the McNaghten formula.

The most important part of the case would be the psychiatric testimony, but first Charlie's background in school, at work, and at home had to be traced by some twenty-five character witnesses, including his parents, and then there would be an appearance by Charlie himself.

The courtroom was usually filled to its capacity of 150 and many of the spectators were as interested in Charlie as they were in the testimony. During the jury selection, he had maintained a half-smirk, seeming either scornful or bored with the proceedings. But when Gaughan, during his opening statement, said he intended to prove Charlie insane and then added that Charlie's IQ was "only a point or two above an idiot," Charlie clutched the corner of the counsel table and glared. Another time, a character witness, his ex-employer John Hedge, said that Charlie was the dumbest man who had ever worked for him. Charlie turned red, gritted his teeth, and seemed on the verge of leaping out of his chair. During recess he told his mother to get to a reporter and tell his side of the story concerning his employment under Hedge.

Mostly, though, he chewed gum and rocked on the legs of

his chair as friends and ex-teachers discussed his childhood. And once, as Gaughan was reading the various confessions, pointing out their illogic and inconsistency, Charlie went to sleep, or at least pretended to.

On Thursday, May 15, Charlie's mother and father, Guy and Helen Starkweather, were scheduled to testify, but Guy failed to show up and had to be served with a subpoena. The couple came under sharp scrutiny during the trial. Helen seemed like a kind and concerned mother but also appeared tired, nervous, and perhaps defeated by the effort of trying to raise and support eight children largely by herself. Guy, partly because of the stories circulating about his relationship with Charlie, drew considerable public criticism. His unwillingness to cooperate with Charlie's counsel and his friendliness with the prosecution (he was quoted as saying to Elmer Scheele in court, "Way to go, Elmer!") gave some the impression he was more concerned with not having the taint of insanity attached to the family name than he was with the survival of his son.

After Helen had taken the stand, Gaughan asked her, "Are you disappointed with the way the defense is handling this case?"

Sitting stiffly, on the verge of tears, she said that she was. The family's main complaint was the insanity plea.

"You don't feel there is anything mentally wrong with Charlie, is that right?"

"Not at the present time."

Toward the end of the testimony, Gaughan asked her if there was anything in particular she would like to tell the jury.

"Yes, sir. It was right after Charles started going with Miss Fugate. Before that, he was the best of friends with his brother. They were together constantly, no arguing or anything. But soon after he started going with Caril, it seemed like his family was pushed behind and his whole life centered around her.

145

That's the way it seemed to me. He wanted to be with her. She seemed to have a hold on him."

"You think he was a different boy after that?"

"Yes, sir."

Gaughan asked if that wasn't at about the same time Charlie had been hit in the head with a paper baler handle while working in the warehouse of the Western Newspaper Union.

"I think he started going with her just before that, yes."

Mrs. Starkweather was excused and soon Charlie was asked to take the stand. He was wearing a blue sport shirt with an open collar and, except for his hands which trembled slightly, seemed one of the more relaxed of those to testify. He sat leaning forward, listening closely to Gaughan's questions.

"What was your first school?"

"Saratoga."

"Did you have any fights with the other kids?"

"The second day I was there."

"Did you have any other troubles while you were there?"

"Couldn't see the blackboard half the time."

"You don't trust people, do you Charlie?"

"Myself."

"You trust me now a little, don't you?"

"No."

"You're naturally suspicious, aren't you?"

"Yeah."

"You don't like people, do you, Charlie?"

"A little bit."

Later, referring to Charlie having been hit in the head with the paper baler, Gaughan asked if his head had hurt the next day.

"I got drunk that night and it hurt worse."

"What did you do that night?"

"I got pretty well pickled. I don't remember what happened."

"Do you still have headaches?"

"Yeah."

"How often do you have them?"

"Every other day, sometimes."

"Did your mother and father know about them?"

"No. I didn't tell them."

"Did you yell at people on the street while driving in the garbage truck?"

"I'd yell at some old guy and tell him how to drive."

"Why did you kill, Charlie?"

"Self-defense, the ones I killed."

"Do you feel any remorse for the people you killed?"

"I won't answer that."

"Why were you mad at Caril Fugate at the cave?"

"For what she did."

"What did she do?"

"Shot Carol King."

"Do you feel any remorse for the people you killed?"

"I won't answer that."

After a brief cross-examination, Charlie was excused.

On Friday, May 16, as Charlie left the courtroom for noon recess, he lashed out with his free hand, striking a press photographer from Iowa who was trying to take his picture. Some of those who saw the incident believed the photographer shoved his camera in Charlie's face to make him mad and thus get a story. Charlie apologized afterward but then added under his breath: "Next time I'll kick you in the head." Sheriff Karnopp, who was responsible for Charlie and constantly chained to him in public, didn't have a relaxed moment during the entire trial. "I never knew what he was going to try next," he says. "I half expected he would try to make a break for it."

On Monday, May 19, the critical part of the trial, the psychiatric testimony, began. Earlier, in his opening statement, Gaughan had outlined the defense: He would prove that Charlie was suffering from delusions when he killed Jensen and was therefore legally insane. This was not a "who" but a "why" trial, he pointed out, then said that part of Charlie's mental problem centered around the inability to distinguish between "big" and "little" things. For instance, it was much more important to him that he wear a certain kind of shoe to the trial than the fact that he was on trial for his life. He characterized Charlie as an underprivileged, mentally deficient boy and made an unsubstantiated claim that he could have a brain tumor or "pressure on the brain." Now his expert witnesses would confirm most of these claims — something that the twenty-five character witnesses had not seen fit to do.

After finding only one local psychiatrist willing to testify on Charlie's behalf, attorneys Gaughan and Matschullat had had to cast around the country before they finally located a respected psychologist and psychiatrist in Kansas City, Missouri, who agreed to test Charlie and tell the court their findings. One of the experts, Dr. Nathan Greenbaum, partly because he avoided the use of standard medical terminology or "labels," seemed verbose and lost the attention of some people in the courtroom. His testimony, reproduced here in part, is considerably edited: "My conclusions, based on my observations and examinations, lead me to the opinion that Charles Starkweather is suffering from a severe mental disease or illness of such a kind as to influence his acts and has prevented him from using the knowledge of right and wrong at the time of commission of such an act.

"A number of important facts were found. One of the very important things which I found was that he is suffering from a severe warping of the emotional faculties; that is, he is unable to experience feelings that other people do. People don't mean anything to him. They are no more than a stick or a piece of wood to this boy."

Greenbaum went on to say that Charlie was completely detached from other people and that he did not have the ability that most people have to control anger — that the moment he had an impulse, he acted upon it. The doctor stated that had the boy been brought to his office before the murder spree occurred, the warning signs would have been so apparent that he would have said, "This person is dangerously sick and has to be put under maximum security because he is dangerous."

In regard to Charlie's perceptions, Greenbaum stated: "He tends to perceive things in a somewhat distorted way. He will pick out things which are not important because of his particular way of looking at things. The act of killing meant to him no more than stepping on a bug. You can take a creature out of a jungle and tame him and maybe develop a surface crust of being domesticated . . . but . . . the crust is only on the surface, and it can break through under much less provocation than a creature who is thoroughly domesticated and has always been. It is further true that when such a creature tastes blood it breaks through and a wild rampage occurs in which a primitive impulse comes back."

Near the end of his testimony, Dr. Greenbaum refused on cross-examination to define Charlie's mental illness, saying he didn't believe in the use of definitions in psychology: "I would be very glad to make up a name for it. We could call it ABC. There is no single word at this time that describes every manifestation of this disease. Giving a name to it would not make it appear suddenly, and not giving a name to it won't make it disappear. Say I have a bookcase that is full of books. You can say you're going to put all the tall books together, or all the short books together, and all the medium-sized books together. That would be one way, but it still wouldn't tell you much about what the books are like . . . If you're interested in any one book, you still have to look in that one."

The next to testify was Dr. John O'Hearne, the psychiatrist

from Kansas City. He had given Charlie a physical examination and began by discussing his findings: "The result of the physical and neurological examination, a special examination of his nervous system, disclosed a short, stocky young fellow with breasts somewhat large but muscularly developed, with tenderness in the spot where we usually expect it to be if a peptic ulcer is present, with a hole in his left eardrum, which apparently has been there quite a long time, with decreased deep tendon reflexes — the one where the doctor hits you in the knee and the foot flies up. Charlie's hardly moved on examinations such as these."

O'Hearne went on to comment on how easily Charlie flushed, how easy it was to upset him, how afraid he was of being examined. The doctor found his subject defective in that he could not perform well under stress. "If things would come at him one at a time, slowly as in a routine job, he would be able to handle these things, but if things began to flood in on him such as the work not going right, the sprinkler in the ceiling coming on, or somebody yelling and a whistle going all at once, I don't think he could function . . . he would be like a frightened animal." Charlie was in this state, O'Hearne believed, when he committed the murders.

The doctor finished by saying that Charlie had never completely developed into a human being. "Yes, he walks around in the body of a human being, but the thoughts and the feelings are not there like they are in an ordinary person, who has learned by being around others and has feelings for them, with them, and in relation to them. This is the way we learn to be people. I don't.think he has ever learned to be a person . . . Words come easily, and I think they come correctly, to Charlie — but perhaps I could illustrate with an example. On the continuing examination here this morning, when I asked him how he liked what was going on, he said he didn't like it. I said, 'What would you like to do about it?' He said, 'If I had a grenade I would show you.' I said, 'What?' He said, 'A bomb.' I said, 'What would you do with a bomb?' He said, 'I would kill Greenbaum with it.' I said, 'What would you do with the other people in the courtroom?' He said, 'To hell with them.' Anybody that says something that he disagrees with, like his ex-boss there, he wants to shoot him. He wants to bomb them. He wants to bomb Greenbaum."

The last psychiatric witness for the defense was Dr. John Steinman, the one Lincoln psychiatrist who agreed to testify. Steinman, a short, dark-haired man with dark eyes and a low, well-modulated voice, was effective, striking people as being "deep" and "tremendously intelligent."

Near the beginning of Steinman's testimony, Gaughan asked him, "Now, Doctor, based on your examination and findings, is the diseased mind of the defendant, as you have described, such that he is unable to adapt himself to the realities of the society with which he is in contact?"

Steinman: "Yes, I believe that is true. Perhaps I can best illustrate that with a statement he made to me when I first interviewed him. In talking about his eyesight, his marksmanship, he said, 'I'm not as good a shot as they say I am. One thing though, I am quick on the draw.' He said, 'That is no good. I get that from watching television.' He said, 'That is no good even for a lawman because there is no use you can do with it, being quick on the draw, except for a lawman.' "

Gaughan: "Is it or is it not true that the defendant is unable to feel normal emotions like his fellow human beings with his diseased mind?"

Steinman: "I would say that his range of emotions is limited, that he feels perhaps two that we are familiar with: anger and fear, or anxiety. The other shadings of emotions — pity, sympathy, the feeling of attachment for another individual (for the entire person and not just a quality or an attribute of them) is something I think he is striving for but actually only has a dim recognition of . . . . When I asked him what happened and how he felt through this when he committed these acts, he has always come back with the same thing: 'Self-defense.' I said, 'Self-defense, how is that?' He said, 'Haven't you ever felt what it is like to have a cop chasing you?' He will admit fear but if I were to say he was yellow or a coward he would get angry."

Steinman went on to say that Charlie sincerely believed his actions were justified through self-defense. "One of Charlie's problems," said Steinman, "is that he is unable to fully appreciate the value of human life. He thinks he can feel close to certain people — he feels loyal and protective toward them — but he is incapable of feeling closeness with the depth and complexity of a fully developed human being . . . . I think he would be a child of five or six with a cap gun in a time of stress or strain with a gun. 'Bang, you're dead.' It means just about that much to him."

Gaughan: "We have testimony given by family and friends about Chuck's behavior during and after the murders that he was happy, cheerful, gay, no different than before. What would that indicate?"

"I would say that it would indicate a diseased mind. A person who had committed the act of killing three people including a young child and then returned to friends and family and appeared to be normal and cheerful was not able to feel things the way other people would."

"What about all his fights?"

"I believe this has something to do with his sense of self-esteem, the way he sees himself as an individual. He wants to have a certain amount of self-respect. He was doing poorly in school in many things . . . ."

Elmer Scheele was effective during his cross-examination of the defense psychologist and psychiatrists. They admitted to him that Charlie had demonstrated an ability to plan and reason when he stole Robert Jensen's car and when he called Marion

Bartlett's place of work before killing him. They admitted that his mental problems did not fall within the narrow definition of legal insanity. Like Greenbaum, the others admitted that they could not give a name such as schizophrenia to his illness or disease.

Now that the defense had claimed insanity, the burden of proof shifted to the prosecution. They had to demonstrate that Charlie was legally sane — and they were prepared. The psychiatric testimony for the state began on Tuesday afternoon and was completed Wednesday morning. Three witnesses, a Lincoln psychologist and two Lincoln psychiatrists, all testified that they had tested Charlie and found that he had a personality disorder but was sane. They said that his disorder did not warrant being committed to an institution and, if he were declared insane and committed, he would soon be released to walk the streets again. They had no problem in defining Charlie's problem. Dr. Robert Stein summed it up: "I made the diagnosis that Charles had a personality disorder characterized by emotional instability, considerable emotional insecurity and impulsiveness, that this would fit into a category under the antisocial personality disorder."

They tested his IQ, also, and found it to be 110 — with a score on the performance section of 119. This was thirteen points higher than the defense's test results. Supposedly, a person may rate lower than his actual intelligence on such tests but never higher. They attributed his higher score to the spirit of cooperation he felt for the prosecution; he simply hadn't tried as hard for the defense.

Elmer Scheele knew that the possibility of Charlie soon being back on the street would pale any jury. On Wednesday afternoon he rested his case.

The trial was over except for brief closing arguments which were given the next morning.

Clem Gaughan, a handsome, self-assured man who at one

time considered becoming an actor, changed his technique during his extemporaneous speech. After having been brusque, even rude at times toward witnesses during the trial, he began to sob during part of his final fifty-minute talk. In much the same manner as Humphrey Bogart, playing the defense attorney in the 1949 movie *Knock on Any Door*, he compared his own impoverished background to Charlie's. He said in part, "This boy is a product of our society. Our society that spawned this individual is looking for a scapegoat. Caril Fugate should get the same punishment as this lad, and I can tell you right now that she is never going to get the death penalty. In many ways I think I know this lad as well as anyone alive does. His life, my life, are almost parallels until our nineteenth birthday. I stand here and weep unashamedly. I hated everybody and everything and I could lick anybody. Society treated me exactly as it treated Charles Starkweather." He looked directly at Charlie's father and said, "But the good Lord gave me, possibly, a little better parents."

He turned to the jury and denied the possibility of Charlie ever being released if declared insane. "I assure you that even an act of Congress will not take him out of the state hospital. The society that spawned this young lad has set up rules for the insane."

Gaughan's final statement was an argument against capital punishment. "The Bible commandment which says 'Thou shalt not kill,' " he told the jury, "applies just as much to you as to Starkweather." He said that if they returned the death sentence he would personally arrange to have them witness the execution. "I will take you to the death house so you can see him with his trousers cut to the knees, with his arms bare, his head shaved, with electrodes attached. And when the switch is pulled, you will see the electricity snap and the smoke come from his head, his hair stand on end as the electricity goes through his body. You will see him jerk in the straps and see him fall forward. That is your responsibility, not mine. Ladies and gentlemen, I ask you for the life of Charles Starkweather."

Matschullat also made an impassioned speech, mostly against capital punishment, but he did add that the defense had received no cooperation from Charlie's family. He said, "We don't blame the family — they don't know any better.

"He who sets that boy in the electric chair will have a terrific responsibility," he went on, ". . . there will be days and months in the future when you will wonder about it. This could happen to your son and daughter. We are not here so much to save Charlie but to see that other boys and girls will have a chance for a fair trial, representation. Think of the men we rehabilitate after a war. If you can do it for millions, you can do it for one other — a brethren of your own community. The state's case has made Charlie out as eligible to be an officer in the U.S. Army. That's ridiculous! Saying he was a 'friendly lad,' 'cheerful,' 'cooperative,' with 'an IQ of 110,' a little better than the average — yours and mine!"

Toward the end, he said, "Are we going to push this boy down in the electric chair if he has a deranged mind? Why should we kill the boy? Let's kill the devil in him!"

Elmer Scheele and Dale Fahrnbruch both made speeches for the prosecution. Scheele, a slim, soft-spoken man, had a dramatic effect, too, but he achieved it by speaking quietly, thoughtfully. Recognized for his ability as a prosecutor, and for his logic and sense of ethics, he was possibly the most respected, popular man in the courtroom. He said, referring to Gaughan's speech, "That was one of the most emotional appeals I have ever heard. Such appeals are common when you have a weak case, or no case at all. Then you must distract the jury's attention from the facts. I've got to rely entirely on you twelve ladies and gentlemen to judge this case on the facts in evidence. It is unfair and ridiculous to attempt to place the blame on society and ask you to do nothing as far as Charles Starkweather, because the blame is on society. Let us get back to earth, get our feet on the ground . . . if justice is to be accomplished and society is to be given the protection it deserves. His own parents will tell you he acted perfectly normal. Can't you see what a hoax it is to persuade you into grasping at the straw of insanity? Starkweather is a man who can never be safely released upon society again. This jury has to go all the way to protect this community — our families, yours and mine — from the defendant."

And Fahrnbruch talked of the claim by the defense that Starkweather could not operate under stress: "Yet he made six decisions when he shot Robert Jensen, a decision every time he pulled the trigger. Every possible fact relative to the Jensen case that is capable of corroboration from physical facts backs up Starkweather's statements. Yet the defense does not want you to believe him. You the jury must decide what protection you are going to give this community. Do you want evidence of malice? Remember the picture of Jensen's head. Do you want intent? What about the shotgun sawed off because it would spread more? Self-defense? It would be more accurate to term it self-preservation to avoid detection and apprehension."

Court was adjourned. It took the jury almost twenty-four hours to return a guilty verdict for first-degree murder on both of two counts. They specified the death penalty.

After the verdict was in, Guy Starkweather said, "The Lord giveth and the Lord taketh away."

Chapter EIGHT

SOMETIME after Charlie's capture, a list of his admitted crimes was released by the Lincoln *Star*.

Armed robbery (Dec. 1 at Crest service station).

Attempted safe burglary or robbery (at Crest station).

Assault (simple, common, felonious, aggravated, with deadly weapon; and battery, with intent to do great bodily harm).

Unlawful transportation of a dead body (Bartletts' bodies and others moved).

Forcible entry.

Petty larceny and grand larceny.

Mayhem.

Inciting to riot, and disturbing the peace.

Auto theft.

Discharging firearms within the city limits.

Carrying concealed weapons (knife and .32 cal. pistol).

Possession of shotgun with sawed-off barrel.

Unlawful flight to avoid prosecution.

Contributing to the delinquency of a minor.

Accessory (before, after, and during the commission of a felony).

Perjury.

Execution of a false document (conflicting confessions).

Destruction of private property.

Destruction of evidence and mutilation of a body.

Violation of Dyer Act (transporting stolen auto across state line).

Violation of Mann Act (woman across state line for immoral purposes).

Violation of Smith Act (gun across state line for illegal purposes).

Speeding (over 110 mph in Wyoming chase).

Resisting arrest.

Reckless driving and running a red light (Douglas).

Charlie admitted to at least thirty-seven criminal actions, and there were many lesser law violations too numerous to mention. This overwhelming tally, committed by someone who, until that time, had only been apprehended for minor traffic violations, cried out for an explanation, and everyone from ministers to magazine writers seemed to have one. The day after Charlie's trial, which had received nationwide coverage, J. Edgar Hoover made a public announcement urging a "nationwide crackdown" to halt the rise of juvenile crimes. He said that "muddled sentimentalists" and "confused psychiatrists" must bear much of the blame for the teen-age crime problem. Lincoln Police Chief Joe Carroll concurred with Hoover, but the two Kansas City doctors, Greenbaum and O'Hearne, denounced his statement. Greenbaum said, "It's not a matter of being hard or soft on the juveniles. You can crack down on the immediate crisis but like weeds it will spring up again sometime in the future." O'Hearne said, "We've been cracking down since recorded history and crimes still haven't stopped. The

youth crisis was reflected by Latin authors 2,000 years ago."
And Greenbaum concluded, "The Hoover statement doesn't get
to the root of the problem of why crimes are committed. No
future Starkweather will be deterred because you kill Charlie
Starkweather. These crimes do not arise from a vacuum."

Lincoln once was called "Holy City" because it was thought
to have more churches per capita than any other city on earth,
and predictably, Charlie became the subject of numerous ser-
mons. The Lincoln school system took a hard look at itself and
didn't like what it saw. Teachers had realized that Charlie had
problems but they didn't know how serious they were; his behavior didn't interfere with school routine so he was never referred to the school psychologist. A trained counselor might
have spotted Charlie and helped him, but such a person was
then unknown to the Lincoln system.

Charlie's parents were easy targets but they, themselves,
could see nothing wrong with the way they had raised Charlie.
His father, Guy, said he thought of himself and Charlie as
being "close." Yet his doors were locked when Charlie went on
his rampage: "I thought maybe he'd come home, and I don't
think Charlie would have hesitated to shoot me. They say a
man will not go against his own flesh and blood, but that's not
the case now." He finally said in exasperation: "I'm tired of
taking the blame for this. What could I have done? . . . He
was old enough to make his own decisions. If he had only
come to us with his problems."

James Reinhardt spent many hours interviewing Charlie and
came to the conclusion that killing both served his immediate
needs and symbolized the overcoming of opposing forces.
Though Charlie had a deep sense of failure and inadequacy, he
wanted more than anything to be powerful and important.
Reinhardt believed his physical mannerisms — such as a withdrawn look and appearing not to hear when someone spoke to
him — were ways to shield this feeling of inadequacy. But in-

side he was full of fantasies of power, and these fantasies became so real at times that he could not tell if he were asleep or
awake. The gun, said Reinhardt, was a poor defeated ego's
short road to power.

But how did Charlie come to be that way?

Charlie's lawyers, Gaughan and Matschullat, contacted the
Menninger Clinic in Topeka, Kansas, to see if a complete psy-
chiatric study might be performed. The clinic agreed — but
only if Charlie could be put completely in their care for as long
as necessary, perhaps months. "We had to give up the idea,"
Gaughan says. "There was no way in the world the state of
Nebraska was going to let Charlie out of its hands for that long."
They did the next best thing and had as many tests performed in
Lincoln as time and Charlie would permit. Even though Charlie wasn't proven to be legally insane, those test results probably
provided more clues to understanding him than anything else.
Statements made by the defense witnesses indicated failure by
nearly everyone who touched Charlie's life. Two key statements, made by O'Hearne and Steinman, seem of particular
significance.

O'Hearne: "I think the family environment didn't teach him
to be an ordinary person. I think the person he fears most,
reasonably or unreasonably, is his father, and this is something
that to other people might seem unnatural — that his father
who has been incapacitated from work for years from arthritis is
the man who to him was the biggest threat. I think he has certain mixed feelings toward his parents. I think he has loyalty
for them. I think also there is a deep down anger and hostility.
I think that his subsequent actions point out what some of these
feelings might have been. I think he took out on other people
some of his feelings he may have had toward his own family."

Steinman: "He was doing poorly in school in many things.
I think some of them might have been preventable or remedia-

ble . . . His difficulty with spelling and writing represent certain types of disorders that are found during early school years which might have been helped. These problems made him feel inferior and made him need to feel his adequacy in other ways . . ."

Charlie's parents, not the doctors, pointed out the change that had come over Charlie once he started going with Caril Fugate. It is known that sociopaths — the term the expert witnesses for the prosecution used and one which fits Charlie's behavior — can function reasonably well in a structured environment, but once they fall into a more permissive one — such as becoming a gang member — they are more likely to commit antisocial acts. Caril, according to Charlie at least, liked and condoned everything he did. When he aligned himself with her, it must have done a great deal to allow him to express his hatred.

Reinhardt believed that Charlie could not feel deeply for anyone. His changing attitude toward Caril after their capture is an indication that it may be true. As long as she had a quality he liked — in this case her adoration of him and her permissiveness — he was fiercely loyal. But when she abandoned him, possibly for her own survival, he was through with her. There are inmates in prisons over the country who have "taken the rap" for friends, lovers, wives, husbands, and though this was Charlie's plan he was unable to carry it out. Once the quality he liked in Caril was gone, he came to hate her as much as he hated everything else — as the days leading up to and through her trial demonstrated. The testimony he made in court against her, something he did not have to do, is one of the reasons she is in prison today.

Caril's trial for the murder of Robert Jensen was held in late October, four months after Charlie was sentenced to die. In some ways it was the simplest of all the murders to try her for. No one was claiming that she helped Charlie kill Jensen — but she did help rob the boy, which made her an accomplice and under law equal in guilt. Still, the Jensen case was a poor choice in that it did not confront the issue of Caril's possible direct involvement in some of the other murders.

In many ways the two trials were similar — many of the same witnesses gave much the same testimony. Caril's trial was extraordinary in that she was the youngest female in the history of the country to be tried for first-degree murder, and it was different from Charlie's in the sense that her lawyer was claiming innocence, and not innocence by reason of insanity. Since any statements she might have made before her trial possibly could have been used against her, she had not had to testify at Charlie's trial, but Charlie was asked to testify at hers. He could not be forced to, of course, as there was nothing with which to force him: he was scheduled to die on December 17.

Back during Charlie's trial, a much-quoted line, attributed to him, was that if he fried in the electric chair then Caril should be sitting in his lap. Charlie claimed that his attorneys dreamed up the line but he went along with it. At her trial, Caril's lawyer, John McArthur, asked Charlie if he still felt the same way. He replied, "No I don't. Now I don't care if she lives or dies."

Charlie, avoiding Caril's glare, retold the story of several of the murders. His testimony completely refuted McArthur's opening statement which had said that Caril was an unwilling hostage who had gone with Charlie because she feared for the lives of her parents. The question was: Would the jury believe him? Elmer Scheele was betting they would.

Scheele asked Charlie, "Was Caril Fugate there when you did these things to Mr. and Mrs. Bartlett?"

"I didn't see her when I shot Mr. Bartlett, no."

"But she was in the house?"

"Yes."

"And was she in the same room when you shot Mrs. Bartlett?"

"Yes."

"And was she in the same room when you threw the knife at Betty Jean?"

"Yes."

"Now, then, what did you do after this all happened there at the Bartlett home?"

"I cleaned it up."

"When you were cleaning up, what was Caril Fugate doing?"

"Watching TV."

Charlie, whose story in court corresponded with the statement he gave to Dale Fahrnbruch, repeated how Caril had grabbed the gun from his hand, saying she was going to blow her mother's head off, repeated how Caril had held a gun on Carol King and had taken Robert Jensen's billfold. He told how he and Caril were frequently separated, that she had several chances to escape, but that she had never tried to get away.

Charlie remained cool despite McArthur's efforts to rattle and confuse him. McArthur noticed Charlie wasn't wearing his glasses and said, "Charles, is it hard for you to see from where you are? "

"I can see."

"Can you see Caril Fugate?"

"Yes."

"And you could see better if you had them on?"

"Yes . . . I don't feel like putting them on."

"Charles, would you rather not see what's going on here?"

"There ain't nobody in here that I want to see."

At one point, McArthur began reading the statement Charlie made to Elmer Scheele soon after being captured. In it Charlie had maintained that Caril was his hostage. McArthur stopped reading and said, "Do you recall that?"

"That's what I said, but it ain't true. That whole statement is a bunch of hogwash."

McArthur asked if Caril had known that he committed the Colvert murder. Charlie said she knew he had been present. McArthur asked if he ever thought about what he would do if Caril alerted authorities during their flight. Charlie said, "I wasn't worried about her talking. She wasn't going to talk. I didn't think about what she might have done because I knew she wouldn't talk. She was too worried about being caught."

Then Elmer Scheele, referring to the statement Charlie had given him, said, "Now, Charles, why did you not tell the entire truth to me when I asked you questions about those matters?"

"I told you that once before."

"Well, will you tell me now?"

"I was protecting Caril Fugate."

Charlie's time in court was finished. He had done his job. He was in a good mood about it — as he had been all during his two days of testimony. On the way to the courthouse one day, the driver of the car he was in had pulled into the parking lot and bumped into the concrete foundation of the old building. Charlie said nothing for a while but when they were on the elevator in the courthouse, he turned to the driver and said, "Where'd you get your license? Sears and Roebuck?"

If there were some jurors who didn't believe Charlie's testimony, there was witness after witness they could believe who had seen Charlie and Caril on their trip and said that Caril could have escaped if she had tried.

Gertrude Karnopp took the stand and related to the court her conversations with Caril in the car on the way back to Lincoln. She told about Caril's apparent unconcern that she was wearing Clara Ward's jacket and about the newspaper clippings Caril had in her pocket. Today, Mrs. Karnopp says, "I was matron in charge of Caril during the trial, but we had another woman along, too. The reason was, we were a little concerned about what Caril might do when I testified. What she did do was get in a staring contest with me. She wouldn't take her eyes off me for a second after I testified. Finally, we went to the restroom, and when she stared at me in there, too, I told her, 'Caril, you don't have to keep looking at me like that. All I did was tell the truth, and you know it.' "

Probably most damaging of all was the testimony of Wyoming deputy sheriff William Romer, who said that Caril told him she had seen her family murdered. And Caril's own testimony was unconvincing; she seemed hostile, kept getting her story mixed up, and had frequent lapses of memory.

In the closing arguments, Elmer Scheele did not ask for the death penalty, but he did ask for a conviction of first-degree murder for the robbery-slaying of Robert Jensen. He said in part, "Even fourteen-year-old girls must recognize they cannot go on eight-day murder sprees. We have leaned over backward to give this girl a fair trial. Now, ladies and gentlemen, the time has come when she must face the consequences of her conduct. This fourteen-year-old girl is guilty of first-degree murder as charged. We must convince persons of all ages they will be caught, tried, and punished if they break the law."

The verdict, like Charlie's, was returned in twenty-four hours. Caril was guilty of first-degree murder on the second count, murder while in the perpetration of a robbery. The sentence was life imprisonment.

One member of the jury told what she had gone through to condemn a child to life without freedom: "I feel that was the hardest job I have ever been called on to perform. I have a son who will soon be fifteen years old and my heart went out to Caril. From the time this happened last January, I took Caril's side. I made many of our friends disgusted with me because I said they would have to prove to me that she was guilty before I would believe it. I couldn't see how a fourteen-year-old could possibly be that bad . . . Nobody but the jury knows how we thrashed out this evidence and tried our best to find her innocent. There was no doubt in our minds as to her guilt. I for one certainly did not want to serve on that jury. Maybe all of us are a little to blame for what happened. We don't pay enough attention to teen-agers and their problems . . ."

Caril went off to begin her life sentence at the Nebraska Center for Women at York, and Charlie went back to the State Penitentiary for the few months left to him. They were the most productive and possibly the happiest moments of his life.

There is no death row, as such, at the Nebraska prison and Charlie kept his private 8' x 12' cell in the prison hospital. He was in solitary but not in solitude. He had special visiting rights, there was always a friendly guard to talk to, a TV in the corridor, a daily newspaper, and he usually got what he wanted in the way of books, pencil and paper, and art supplies. He spent his days reading, writing, drawing, and gazing out the window. And he made, he claimed, peace with God. To his eight-year-old brother, Greg, he wrote:

Dear Greg:
thank you for letting ne read your book there's a lot of pictures in it and its a very nice book. But when you get older read the Bible it tells more about the Lord from the first of life to the end of life. but do not think that there is a end in the life of the Lord. cause there is no end, he is all ways a live. "to help you." . . . and do this for ne to — be nice to mom and dad and do all you can to help your mother. OK.

Your brother
Charles

To his parents, he wrote this letter, edited by the Lincoln *Journal:*

"Holding on to my life is like trying to hold a handful of sand. If death is still inevitable, God will triumph. Man may take my life, but my soul belongs to Him.

"All my hopes now are of staying alive and repenting for the wrongs I have committed. Killing is a terrible sin against God and man. I hope that someday killing and the taking of human life, even in war, will only be a terrible memory."

While appeals were being made in his behalf, Charlie wrote around 200 manuscript pages of his autobiography. He was writing it, he said, "so others won't make the same mistake," but Reinhardt believed he was writing it to secure his place in history. The professor acted as his agent. As crudely as Charlie wrote, every word he put on paper was precious to him and he was upset when Reinhardt told him it was unlikely that his work would ever be published exactly as he wrote it. Charlie was already looking beyond to a possible extended literary career in the future. If his sentence were commuted to life, he planned to write a novel about murder.

He did, in fact, have some literary success. Part of his story sold to *Parade* magazine for a thousand dollars — money which was doled out for the support of his parents over a six-month period. Much of the rough power of Charlie's writing was lost in the heavy editing, and the material selected was presented in such a way that the message had a hollow ring to it. The piece ended like this:

"Today, after a year of imprisonment, I can count my life in hours. I have had a great deal of time for thought and to retrace back over my life. I hold no fear for the electric chair, it is the price I am paying for taking the lives of others. But bringing my life to an end does not answer why certain things took place. Going to the electric chair will bring to an end my search for answers that are hard to find.

"Now I feel no rebellion toward anything or anyone, only

love and peace. I received this love and peace through the Bible.

"And if I could talk to young people today I would tell them to go to school, to go to Sunday school, to go to church and receive the Lord Jesus Christ as your own personal Savior. Our God is a kind God. He'll forgive and accept you as one of His even if your heart is black and heavy with sin.

"And I would say to them to obey their parents or guardians, and stay away from bad influences, and never undertake anything that you don't understand, and if in doubt don't do it. And most of all don't ever let your intentions and emotions overpower you.

"If I had followed these simple rules, as I was advised to do many times, I would not be where I am today."

Charlie's mother and father, his brothers and sister came to see him often and tried to bring him things he needed. His father, though, seemed to people at the prison to be as infatuated with Charlie's infamy as Charlie was himself. He began hanging around to strike up conversations with other visitors, always introducing himself as "Charlie Starkweather's father." Once he walked into the deputy warden's office with a number of small strips of paper. He asked permission to get Charlie's signature on the pieces of paper so he might sell them to help cover legal expenses. He also wanted to cut off locks of Charlie's hair for the same purpose. Deputy Warden Greenholtz told him he thought it would be inappropriate.

If Charlie's relationship with his father was not what it might have been, he perhaps found a surrogate father in prison — one of his guards, Mike Shimerda, who spent eight hours a day and five days a week with him for his year-and-a-half stay at the penitentiary. Today, Shimerda is sixty-three years old, retired, and spends considerable time at one of two bars in the tiny town of Swanton, Nebraska. He has a beer belly and a florid face but is still a powerful, energetic man, who, despite being small, is given a lot of room by his rowdy drinking buddies. Shimerda has been used to violence all his life; it was an integral part of his career, and his views of Charlie are less judgmental than those who deal with violence in the abstract. They got along well; being on opposite sides of the prison bars did not limit the relationship but defined it in a way that Charlie seemed to need.

In one of the bars in Swanton, drinking beer with whiskey chasers, Shimerda reflects:

"When he first came in, I wouldn't have thought nothing about pulling the switch on him myself because of all the things he did, all the people he killed. But I changed. He was the best inmate I ever dealt with. You hear about his temper, and he had one all right, but he damn well controlled it in the pen — and that was more than you can say for the others in there. Those guys made Charlie look like a baby. They all had more of a temper than he did. They'd flip out and come at you with a knife and everything else. Personally, I think if Charlie had had a decent home life he'd have never done the things he did . . . I can't help but think that if somebody had just paid attention to Charlie, bragged on his drawing and writing, all of this might not have happened."

Shimerda goes on to say that if Charlie was crazy then he, Shimerda, was crazy and so were his three children. He bases this, of course, on casual observation of Charlie functioning in a controlled situation. But he adds: "Charlie did say some things that would make you wonder. One time he said he'd like to get up in the guard tower with the machine guns and just cut loose. Then he said he wished he could get out for just a couple of hours — there were a couple more people he'd like to take care of. But he was always grinning when he said it . . . ."

Shimerda believes that he and Charlie got along because he

never pumped Charlie for information, he accepted him for what he was — a prisoner to be guarded. Because Shimerda didn't pay any attention to Charlie in the beginning, Charlie began to seek him out. "I'd ignore him and he didn't like it. Pretty soon he'd say, 'Hey, Mike, come over here.' I'd say, 'Whaddya you want?' He'd say, 'I'm writing this book. I wanta see what you think about it.' I'd say, 'You know it's against the goddamn rules. I ain't supposed to read that shit you're writing.' Then after a little bit he'd ask how to spell something. I'd say, 'Jesus Christ, you got a dictionary in there — look the sonofabitch up.' Well, over a period of six months, the more I ignored him, the more he wanted to talk."

Shimerda remembers how hungry Charlie was for attention — and how he loved publicity. He always had a eye on the TV in the corridor outside his cell for some mention of him. One of his biggest pleasures was going through the paper and finding his name in it. He never cared what was said about him; as long as he was mentioned at all, he was happy.

The retired guard finishes his recollections by mentioning his last encounter with Charlie. "Just before he fried, he gave me a picture he had drawn and said, 'Mike, I want you to have this to remember me by.' It was a picture of a little boy holding a teddy bear. He said, 'I won't be here tomorrow when you come back to work so I want you to have it.' Goddamn. That was a hell of a feeling. I broke down and cried. And I'm not one to show my emotions either. There's only two times in my life that I can remember crying — when they fried Charlie and the day my own son graduated from West Point and shook hands with the President."

Another prison official who was close to Charlie was Deputy Warden John Greenholtz. Today, Greenholtz sits in an office in the state capitol building. He is chairman of the Nebraska Parole Board — and one of the advocates of Caril Fugate's re-

lease. After a long career in penology, he is an eminently practical man, at once brusque and sentimental. He has memories
of Charlie but few theories. He says simply: "I was his keeper."

From a desk drawer he takes a small prison Bible Charlie
gave him as a memento and a stack of Charlie's mail. "He got
thousands of pieces of mail," Greenholtz says. "Mostly crank
mail, fan mail, and religious tracts. Here's one that says Charlie
was victim of a 'sound detection conspiracy,' whatever that is.
He got some mail from teen-agers — any rumors you may have
heard that he had a teen-age following are true. I remember I
had to throw one teen-age girl out of my office. She insisted
she had to visit Charlie. She said, 'You can't keep me from
seeing him. He's a child of God!' But most of the people who
came to see him wanted to pray with him."

Greenholtz puts the Bible and letters away and rummages
briefly through his desk for some drawings. "I don't see any of
them now, but I have a number of drawings Charlie gave me.
He was always a model prisoner — he used his time construc-
tively — and he developed considerably as an artist while he
was there. He went from simple pencil drawings to Crayola to
water color and finally to oil. I paid for a lot of his art supplies
out of my own pocket. Just before he was sent to the electric
chair, he was working on an elaborate battle scene, a Civil War
scene, I believe, with a large number of soldiers in it. It was
very good, one of the best things he had done, but none of the
soldiers had faces. I told him he should go ahead and finish it
before his time ran out but he never did. When he went to the
chair, all the faces on the soldiers were still blank."

Meanwhile, legal battles on Charlie's behalf, which would
last over a year, were getting under way. His attorneys immediately filed for a new trial, listing seventeen reasons for one, but
were turned down. The second step was to take the case to the
Nebraska Supreme Court, which they did, causing the execu-

tion date to be postponed until March 27, 1959. The state upheld the local court decision and a request for a rehearing was denied.

There was talk of appealing to the federal courts but such a court case would cost around $10,000, so Charlie went in another direction: he applied for a hearing before the State Board of Pardons and Paroles, hoping for clemency. This resulted in the execution date being again postponed.

Then Charlie unexpectedly "fired" his attorneys, writing Judge Spencer that he no longer wanted their services. Since the state had already paid the attorneys anyway, and they would now be working for nothing, his request was honored. He would ask for clemency on his own.

Pale and trembling, he crossed the prison grounds to the parole board meeting room and addressed the board. He said he was sorry for what he had done, and if he could bring his victims back to life he would. Before the murder spree he didn't think so much of life but now he did. He had changed his way of thinking, mostly by reading the Bible. He said that he sincerely felt that if he had been represented properly he would have been given a life sentence. Guy and Helen Starkweather also testified on their son's behalf, along with Ferris Fitzpatrick of Lansing, Michigan, who had appeared out of nowhere. Fitzpatrick explained to the board how, in a dream, he had seen five funnel clouds in the sky at the time of Charlie's murder spree. Fitzpatrick was dismissed. Charlie's plea for clemency was denied. The new date of execution was set for May 22.

Meanwhile, Caril, who was trying for a new trial, was claiming that Charlie had given false testimony because Elmer Scheele had promised to get him a life sentence in return. Everyone denied it, but as Charlie's new date to die approached, Caril asked the governor that Charlie be given another stay of execution "so he will have plenty of time to tell the truth." Her request was turned down and she asked to see Charlie, to talk to him "in front of a minister." He refused to see her and she wired President Eisenhower.

"I am now 15 years old. About a year and a half ago on a day when I was in public school, 19-year-old Starkweather who I had told several days before in front of my mother never to see me again went into my house and killed my 2-year-old baby sister, mother and stepfather. Starkweather later confessed I had nothing to do with his murder which is true. Later he changed his story and said I helped him do his murder which is not true. He forced me to go with him when I got home from school against my will. Starkweather will be executed tomorrow. I have been denied by Governor Brooks a request to see him and see if he will tell the truth in front of a minister or someone else who would be fair before he is executed. I know of no one else to turn to because all of my family I was living with he killed. I know you are very busy but please help me in any way you can."

One of Eisenhower's counsels replied: "The Starkweather case is entirely a state matter. The President has no jurisdiction or authority in any way to comply with your request."

In the early hours of the morning of May 22, 1959, Charlie, who had given up writing his book a few days before because there was no hope of finishing it, had part of his head shaved so the electrode could make proper contact, enjoyed a steak for his last meal, and prepared to die at 6:00 A.M. He was calm and ready. A minister was with him. The witnesses had arrived at the prison. Then, ninety-eight minutes before the switch was to be thrown, Charlie was given a stay of execution. Guy Starkweather had called a federal district judge in Omaha, finally asking that the case be appealed to the federal courts. Charlie grinned and shook the attending minister's hand.

⟩rieve enraged those who wanted to see Charlie dis-
⟩fast and as cheap as possible. Robert Ruark, for in-
⟩, wrote in his syndicated newspaper column: "Something — I use the word advisedly — named Charles Starkweather has been granted a stay of execution for a fit of whimsy
in which he managed to kill by gun and knife exactly 11 persons. You cannot blame the little monster's father for trying everything to save the little monster with the street corner haircut
and the bed-room-eyes-cum-droopy-cigaret . . . Anything
with a face like Starkweather's literally belongs in a bottle in a
medical museum. But creep that he is, I claim that undue cru-
elty in the name of the law has been administered to Charles
Starkweather . . . An eleventh-hour reprieve, which gives
him two more weeks of torment, is not nice even for a mad
dog."

Three court-appointed lawyers helped with the appeal but a
panel of judges turned it down. There would be no more court
hearings, they said, and refused to extend the stay of execution.
The new death date was June 12.

Suddenly, a Washington, D.C., lawyer, James J. Laughlin,
appeared, saying he would represent Charlie, and helped Guy
Starkweather write an application for a writ of habeas corpus. A
two-week stay of execution was granted as a result, making June
25 the new execution date. The sixty-one-year-old Laughlin,
who defended "Axis Sally" in the famed 1949 sedition trial, said
he was taking the case in the interest of justice and without
compensation. He also said he had plans which would tie up
the case in courts for perhaps two years.

But, unexpectedly, Laughlin's request for a hearing was denied. The execution would be delayed no longer. The embit-
tered lawyer told the press: "I can only say that passion, preju-
dice and public excitement was in full force and vigor and
prevented a disposition of the matter in a calm and judicial at-

mosphere. I think the result of this case clearly demonstrates what Chief Justice Hughes said a number of years ago that the law favors the man with the bulging pocketbook. Had Starkweather had means there would have been no difficulty in obtaining a Lincoln lawyer to represent him in the last hours of his life." Laughlin concluded by suggesting that foul play had taken place to insure Charlie's death.

On Charlie's last day he was asked to donate his eyes to an eye bank. "Why should I?" he said testily. "Nobody ever gave me anything." He complained to his mother, "I don't feel right. I was okay the last time. I was ready. But now I'm all mixed up."

But when Mike Shimerda got ready to leave, about ten that night, Charlie gave him the picture of the boy and the teddy bear and said, "Don't worry about me, Mike. I died the last time. They can't kill me again."

Today, Shimerda says, "I was plenty shaken when I left the prison. You could feel death in that place. I think every guard, whether they knew Charlie or not, could feel it. Then, when I got to the front entrance, there they were — the whole place was crawling with newspaper people and everybody else. It made me sick. I told this one guy, 'All right, you goddamn vultures. You're finally going to see what you came for.' "

The execution was set for June 25, 1959, shortly after midnight. Charlie's family said goodby to him around ten-thirty on the twenty-fourth and went to his grandmother's house to wait for the news. The prison chaplin, Robert Klein, stayed with him and, at Charlie's request, gave him a small plastic cross to hold while he died. He had spent part of the day using the oil paints Greenholtz had given him to work on the battle scene picture, and it sat, with all its blank faces, drying in the corner.

Thirty minutes before it was time, prison physician B. A. Finkle, who was to pronounce Charlie dead, himself dropped dead of a heart attack in the hall outside the warden's office. The strain of the upcoming ordeal had apparently brought on the attack. The seventy-five-year-old doctor was taken away in the ambulance intended for Charlie. A new doctor and ambulance were obtained and the execution proceeded on schedule.

Several law officers went to the death cell to get him, and one said, "All right, Charlie. It's time to go."

Charlie smiled and said what many believe were his last words: "What's your hurry?" But he quickly went to the cell door, wearing a new blue chambray shirt and jeans for the occasion. He hadn't cared what he wore until he realized there would be newsmen there who would be telling the public what he looked like. The top of his head and his left leg had been shaved earlier that day, for the second time.

The death walk from the prison hospital building to the central building with the electrocution chamber is about a hundred yards along a sidewalk leading across the prison grounds. It was a warm, clear night when Charlie made the walk and the outside lights lit up the grass, the flowers and shrubbery, and the gray mottled walls and guard towers which loomed overhead like a medieval fortress. The Nebraska wind, as usual, was blowing.

Charlie and his escorts proceeded into the main part of the prison. They passed the visitors' room and went through the turnkey's room — a small area between two electronically controlled iron-bar doors — and then down into the basement by way of steep, winding metal steps. Below, the door of the electrocution chamber was solid steel.

Today, the chamber is used to hold racks of cheap civilian suits which are given prisoners upon their release. Charlie was the twelfth and last to make use of the room for its original purpose. The straight-back electric chair, made of simply cut heavy wood, with its seat and back lined with thin rubber matting, is shoved off to one side like a piece of furniture stored in a cellar. There is a stain from a coffee cup on one of the arms, possibly left by an inmate relaxing on a break.

But in 1959, the chair had heavy wires running to it from a shielded control panel. A green curtain was drawn around the upper part of the chair so witnesses would not have to watch the victim's actual moment of death. Over sixty people from around the nation had asked to see Charlie die. Six were required by law to be in attendance. Charlie could have selected three but he waived the right. About forty were actually there, including about twenty newsmen. Behind the covered control panel was the unidentified executioner, an electrician from another state who had been paid $200 and expenses.

At 12:01, the heavy steel door to the room opened and Charlie, flanked by two officers, strode quickly inside and sat down, as witnesses said later, "like he was getting into a barber chair." The hard wooden seat must have been as uncomfortable to him as the desks at Saratoga Elementary School, but he was not made to wait long. His pant leg was rolled up, his calf dabbed with a solution to help conduct the electric current, and the curved metal electrode attached. His arms and legs were secured by leather straps. His head was fitted into a headrest on the back of the chair and the solution spread on the shaved area on top. A headpiece, resembling a football helmet and containing an electrode, was placed on his head. Charlie, who could barely make out the crowd of onlookers in the dim light from a single overhead bulb, squinted at them and managed a weak smile.

Greenholtz, who had tears in his eyes from the death of his close friend Dr. Finkle, asked Charlie if he had any last words. Charlie pressed his lips together and shook his head emphatically no. Greenholtz closed the curtain and signaled toward the panel for the man behind it to go ahead.

The switch was pulled three times, making a loud thumping sound each time it sent the 2200 volts through Charlie's body. His short, bow legs could be seen jerking in their straps each time. The first jolt stunned him, the second knocked him unconscious, and the third stopped his heart.

He was pronounced dead at 12:04.

The witnesses were quickly led out by way of steps which went directly up to the grounds outside the prison. As soon as they were gone, the body was placed on a stretcher and covered so it could be carried to the waiting ambulance on the street outside.

For the last half-hour there had been a mild disturbance on that street. Gangs of teen-agers had been cruising by with their radios playing at full volume. Many of them were drinking beer and some had stopped their cars and gotten out. Some had come on foot. The boys were mostly wearing T-shirts and jeans, the girls shorts and cool summer blouses. There were about fifty in all.

Prison guards had tried to keep the crowd moving, but they kept circling and coming back, circling and coming back. Finally the police had to be called in to clear the area so that the body could be removed.

EPILOGUE

CHARLIE'S LIFE ended with his execution, but Caril Fugate's story is not so simply concluded. At this writing, she is thirty-one and is still serving a life sentence at the Nebraska Center for Women at York, fifty miles from Lincoln.

The reformatory, commonly called "York," has for a visitor who is free to come and go a pleasant, tranquil atmosphere. York is sometimes called "The Campus" by those living there, and the three buildings which comprise the living quarters are called "dorms." And York does resemble a small college for girls more than a prison, or perhaps a home for unwed mothers. The grounds are grassy and shaded by many trees. When the weather is nice, there are usually inmates outside taking walks or sitting under the trees reading. There is a swing and other playground equipment for visiting children. Children may stay overnight at the guest house with their inmate mothers. There is a wire fence around the grounds and a lock on the gate —

but the security is more intended to keep people out than in. Everyone has a job — cleaning, cooking, sewing, clerical duties, public service work outside the prison — and those under twenty-five without a high school education are urged to take classes. But there is still a lot of free time, and a library, a canteen, and TV rooms to help fill it. Many girls eventually get TVs, radios, and record players for their own rooms — which can hardly be called cells. They may go in supervised groups into town on bowling and swimming jaunts. On the weekend, live bands sometimes perform in the large lobby of the relatively new North Hall, where Caril lives. It is difficult for some visitors to realize that this is a prison and that the girls lounging about are criminals, even murderers. One might assume that inmates are there because of the minimal nature of their crimes or because they have proven themselves at other, grimmer institutions. In fact, who goes to York is solely a matter of whether the crime was committed in North Dakota, Wyoming, Montana, and Nebraska — the states the reformatory services.

What makes York a prison, of course, is that those who live there have lost their freedom. Supervisor Jackie Crawford believes that further punishment in the form of extreme discipline, harassment, deprivation, and personal degradation is not only inhuman and unnecessary but also thwarts the institution's goal of total rehabilitation.

This has not always been the practiced policy at York. Caril Fugate knows. She has been there longer than any other person, either prisoner or staff member. Until she turned sixteen, she was kept in virtual solitary confinement and experienced all the attending discomforts of isolation. She found the rules in the early years dehumanizing: no talking was allowed except during meals and recreation; morning toiletry was closely supervised; no make-up was allowed; every sanitary napkin had to be accounted for; radios were not allowed and the few magazines available were censored with scissors; even the slightest, unintentional infraction of rules brought punishment; informing was encouraged and was almost the only way to gain favor with those in charge. But Caril learned to obey, to avoid the other inmates, to be inconspicuous, and she survived. Over the years conditions gradually improved until York became the prison it is today.

Caril, apparently, has always been a model prisoner. She has never had a mark against her for misconduct and has taken advantage of every program the reformatory has offered over the years. Despite an abhorrence of school, she worked through correspondence until she received a high school diploma. She became an expert seamstress. She has for years now been involved in local church groups. The day after the first meeting I had with Caril, she passed a final exam for a ninety-hour geriatric aide course she had taken in nearby Henderson, at the Henderson Nursing Home. Since then, she has worked there full-time, commuting from York.

Everyone in an official capacity at York likes Caril and thinks she has developed into a responsible woman who has something to offer society. They think York can do nothing more for her, that it is time — past time — for her to be released.

Efforts to free Caril have been continuous ever since she was incarcerated. Her lawyers, John McArthur and his son James, took a deep personal interest in her case and have fought every legal battle possible in her behalf. John McArthur became her legal guardian. All of their court battles were fruitless, however, and now parole is her only hope for freedom. Because she was convicted for first-degree murder, she was given a life sentence with no provisions for parole. The only recourse in such a case is for a pardon board to commute the sentence from life to a set term of years. In October 1973 the Nebraska Board of Pardons took that step, commuting Caril's sen-

tence to from thirty to fifty years. Because of Caril's perfect prison record she has acquired a considerable
amount of time off for good behavior, making her possibly eligible for release in June 1976.

In 1973, the parole board believed Caril should be paroled,
and probably the pardon board — a separate body — would
have commuted her sentence to a minimum of twenty-five
years, which in effect, would have allowed her to go free immediately. But the victims' families had to be considered, and
some of them are adamantly against Caril's release. Caril was
so convinced of an imminent parole that she had her bags
packed. Public support and sympathy had grown out of an
NBC special about her, "Growing Up in Prison," first shown on
August 29, 1972. The show indirectly cast some doubt on her
guilt. But it also enraged some Lincoln public officials and relatives of the victims.

At Caril's pardon hearing, she had thirty-three character witnesses to testify in her behalf. Five witnesses showed up to op-
pose commutation of her sentence. One was Mrs. Robert Jensen, mother of the seventeen-year-old boy whom Charlie and
Caril were convicted of murdering. Mrs. Jensen's statement at
the hearing said in part: "I feel that people who kill someone in
the heat of anger should be treated quite differently than those
who go on a murder spree for their thrills.

"It seems more compassion is always dealt to the criminal,
and the victims and their loved ones aren't really considered.
Nor is society in general.

"I would question whether a person who could watch such
crimes — let alone participate in them — could ever be really
rehabilitated so they would be safe to be returned to society.
Even if this could be accomplished, she was sentenced to serve
all of her natural life in prison by a jury trial and a fine judge,
now deceased, and I sincerely feel they meant for her sentence

to be carried out and upheld by the courts. And life imprisonment should mean just that — life imprisonment."

To those who spoke out against Caril's release, fifteen years seemed a small price to pay for ten lives. It amounted to a year and a half a person.

Those in favor of commutation of Caril's sentence, like York supervisor Jackie Crawford, feel that life imprisonment without hope of freedom is itself little more than a slow and expensive form of execution. The board's decision was generally viewed as a safe, middle position which, though it did not satisfy either extreme, was an effort to be fair to both.

Caril and I have met twice, the first time in Jackie Crawford's office. When she walked in the room it was a little as if she had stepped out of the pages of the Starkweather manuscript. It was also, for some reason, like meeting someone from the past, perhaps from high school. She seemed somehow snagged in time. She wore jeans and a sweater, was the same tiny size she had been at fourteen, and moved with the same quick energetic walk that had been captured on the TV film clips. She looked about eighteen — until she was close enough to shake hands, when I could see the lines on her face.

After strained conversation about such things as her upcoming geriatric course exam, the way York has changed over the years, the brutal winters, and a trailer house Jackie Crawford was trying to sell, it became apparent that if Caril acted eighteen instead of thirty-one, it was because she was expected to act that way. When Jackie, who is only slightly older than Caril, said, "Caril had a lot to overcome but she's done a terrific job," it was like a mother speaking of her daughter.

Caril spent most of the interview trying to sit and talk properly, as if she thought of herself as a borderline student trying to impress a teacher, praying just to pass. And perhaps nothing else could be expected of her. It was a difficult moment; in a way, I was forcing her to talk. The book was to come out only months before the critical 1976 parole board meeting. The facts presented — what happened in 1958 — would not be favorable, but a comment about who she had become since might be. Caril knows that returning to society will be difficult, but she wants it with a desperation that affects everything she does. She seemed to feel that she had to prove herself to me, but it obviously hadn't been worth her discomfort. I left without a real feeling for her personality. I could say she is polite, animated, cheerful — but beyond limited terms like that, not much.

Nor did the talk result in any new information about what had actually happened in 1958. I hadn't expected it to, of course, but what if it had? What if Caril had said, "I want to tell you everything that happened"? How many would believe a repeated claim of innocence? Or what if she had announced, "I killed six of them myself"? Would anyone have been really surprised? Besides clarifying exactly who did what, would it make other differences? If Caril is guilty of crimes as yet unconfessed, it might be psychologically beneficial for her to admit them. It might even help her chances of being freed, inasmuch as so many people are convinced she was deeply involved and cannot understand how there can be rehabilitation without an admission of guilt.

But regardless of what she did or did not do seventeen years ago, it is her prison record that should be considered now. Every prison official who has dealt with Caril over the years believes she is not the person she was when she accompanied Charlie Starkweather. They feel that she has been punished enough. Critics sometimes say of writers of books like this that we tend to sympathize with the criminal and to forget the victim. But it is to be hoped that we write about criminals in an effort to understand them and what they represent for their times; sympathy is one outgrowth of that understanding. We try not to forget the victim, but we must recognize that the criminal is the victim too.

Some six months later, I paid Caril another visit — but it was as if I was seeing her for the first time. We had corresponded, and she felt that she knew me better now; since we weren't supervised, she seemed to feel she could be more candid.

Caril looked good. She had recently been on a weekend furlough to Grand Island and had returned with the outfit she wore to our meeting — a white leatherette coat trimmed in imitation fur, and a black satin pantsuit with a silver-stud design on the blouse. But I soon discovered that in other ways things weren't going well at all. She had been sick a lot, suffering mostly from colds but also from a shoulder problem which temporarily had forced her to quit her nurse's aid job; her spirits were low.

Jackie Crawford had been trying to find her another less physically demanding job outside the prison but was having difficulty; volunteer work with churches had been one thing but to employ Caril is apparently considered a risk by local businesses. Also, she was bothered by recent incidents at the prison. Another inmate had tried to start a fight with her, which Caril had avoided. But she was still upset about it. She finds it increasingly difficult to get along with the life-styles of the younger inmates. And the system itself is changing. York is experimenting with having inmates evaluate each other's progress, even to recommending each other for furlough. Caril, who grew up under strict supervision, is having trouble adjusting to the new policy. But the main thing bothering her seemed to be the way she had been treated by one of her supervisors. Some drugs were found on the grounds, leading to a prison-wide shakedown of all the rooms. Caril's room, for an unexplained reason, was torn apart in a way that other rooms weren't. She threw a fit, saying that all her efforts over the years had been wasted, that she still wasn't trusted, still hadn't earned the right to be treated with dignity. Now she was worried that her outburst had undermined her chances for parole.

It was an upsetting meeting, and later I talked with Jackie Crawford about it. "She's regressing, I'm afraid," Jackie said. "She's been kept here too long. You can only do so much to a human being before they lose hope, give up."

But whether Caril has been punished enough is a matter for the state to decide at Caril's next parole board hearing, in June of this year.

Recently, I was given a present by Caril, a leather billfold which had been hand-tooled at York by another inmate. I also received a Christmas card with a color picture of herself enclosed. The card, a snowy nature scene covered with glitter, had a brief note inside:

> Just a few lines to let you know
> all is well and I'm still here. Ha ha.
> Just a little joke.

Notes and Sources

Prologue

Obviously, most of this section comes from my own recollections of the fifties. After it was written I wondered if I had drawn too dark a picture of my teen-age life in South Dallas, so I tracked down and called Charles Willingham, a good friend from those days who now helps make weather satellites in California. After hearing the piece, Charlie assured me things had been that bad or worse. He recalled a number of other similiar incidents which confirmed my overall view of our lives then.

Of a number of books I read about adolescent behavior, the one that helped me the most in this section was *The Vanishing Adolescent* by Edgar Z. Friedenberg.

For an initial, overall view of the Starkweather-Fugate case, I referred to the *New York Times, Life, Newsweek, Time,* and the Lincoln *Journal-Star* papers.

Chapter One

I wish to acknowledge the now deceased Dr. James M. Reinhardt for use of information in his book, *The Murderous Trail of Charles*

Starkweather, published in 1960 by Charles C. Thomas (Thomas Books). All passages from Charlie's autobiography — either paraphrased or quoted — which appear in *Starkweather* originally appeared in Reinhardt's book. Though Reinhardt said that what he published of Charlie's writing was unedited, I have noticed some minor discrepancies; for instance, Charlie frequently wrote M's as N's, and this error was corrected in Reinhardt's book. I tried to locate Charlie's original manuscript to see if other editing had been done, but Reinhardt's widow said his files no longer exist.

Other information about Reinhardt's relationship with Charlie comes from the retired prison guard, Mike Shimerda, who witnessed some of the interviews. Also, Marjorie Marlette, staff writer for the Lincoln *Journal,* who knew something of the relationship and was in close contact with the Starkweather family, provided additional information.

Genealogist Karl Starkweather of Plymouth, Michigan, provided the history of the Starkweather family name. In a letter to the people of Lincoln, published by the Lincoln *Journal,* he said that Charlie was the one black sheep bearing the name Starkweather. He pleaded: "Good people of Lincoln! Could you possibly extend toward this writer a moment or two of compassion?"

I spent long hours with Charlie's one-time best friend, Bob Von Busch, both in a bar and in his small frame house on the east side of Lincoln, and he provided a great deal of information about Charlie's teen-age years. After Bob and his first wife, Barbara, were divorced, he remarried and now lives with his second wife and five children, some of whom are from his prior marriage. After a wild teen-age life, Bob now is a settled family man — but he still combs his thinning hair in a popular fifties style and thinks of that time as the "good old days."

In this chapter I made use of information gathered from the Lincoln *Journal-Star* papers, and statements by Charlie taken by Chief Deputy Dale Fahrnbruch and County Attorney Elmer Scheele. I also used information from both trial transcripts — *State of Nebraska* v. *Charles Raymond Starkweather* and *State of Nebraska* v. *Caril Ann Fugate* — and certain exhibits from Charlie's trial.

It should be pointed out that whenever Charlie, Caril, or others are quoted directly, sources for these quotes are generally given. However, when it is relatively clear in context where quotes are from, sources are sometimes omitted for the sake of immediacy in the text. If sources are not given, it may be assumed that quotes are from the various official records listed here, and that these records are readily available for public scrutiny.

Chapter Two

The account of the murder of Robert Colvert is based on the formal statement Charlie gave to County Attorney Elmer Scheele. The description of the Crest service station is from a photo published by the Lincoln *Journal*.

Tracy Kontos, who was a Lincoln teen-ager in the fifties, retraced much of the murder trail with me and provided many details about those days — such as the story about Bloody Mary's and the sign in front of the National Guard Armory.

The list of movies shown in Lincoln during January 1958 are from the microfilm library of the Lincoln *Journal-Star* papers.

Many scenes recreated in this book — such as when Charlie visited his family after the Colvert murder — are from detailed statements made by Charlie or Caril or from those made by witnesses testifying at the trials. Also, some scenes are from newspaper interviews or interviews I had with the participants.

William Fugate's police record is recorded on dockets in the city and county courts in Lincoln. He died in jail in Lincoln while serving a six-month sentence for "contributing to the delinquency of a minor."

In this chapter I made use of information gathered from *Life*, the Lincoln *Journal-Star* papers, *The Robinson Report*, the Omaha *World-Herald*, interviews with Sheriff Merle Karnopp and now-retired Police Lieutenant Robert Henninger, and statements and trial transcripts already mentioned.

Chapter Three

Today, the Belmont section of Lincoln is no longer a slum. Generally, the streets are paved, the houses and yards neatly kept. The block of Belmont Avenue where the Bartletts lived is now a shopping center with a large Jack & Jill supermarket. The tenement house where Charlie rented a room is now gone, as is the Starkweather home.

With the help of Ron Kontos, of the Clerk of District Court office in Lincoln, I was able to inspect some of the murder weapons, including the .22 used to kill Marion Bartlett and the shotgun from which Charlie sawed the barrel at the Bartletts'. I was told by Lancaster County's Public Defender, T. Clement Gaughan, that gun collectors have offered up to $2000 each for these weapons — a price comparable to those obtained at the public auction in Texas of Charles Whitman's murder weapons.

With the cooperation of Ron Kontos, I also was able to study police photos of the interior of the Bartlett house, as well as numerous court exhibits, including the original copy of the "for the law only" letter and other items taken from Charlie and Caril upon their capture. Any original writing I obtained and reproduced of Charlie's is unedited.

In this chapter I made use of a lengthy statement, unsigned, by Caril Fugate, taken by Chief Deputy Dale Fahrnbruch. Autopsy reports were obtained with the help of Attorney General Paul Douglas. I also made use of interviews with now-retired Lincoln Police Chief Joe Carroll, Gertrude Karnopp — and interviews, news sources, statements, and trial transcripts already mentioned.

Chapter Four

I retraced the murder trail around Bennet twice, once at the same time of year as the murder spree and once in the spring. Both times my car got stuck on the lane going down to the old Myer farm. The storm cellar where Carol King and Bob Jensen were killed has been filled in and is now part of a cornfield. Today, Bennet is more of a ghost town than ever; in fact, all the downtown businesses seem to be closed — except the post office and Jensen's General Store. When I stopped in the store to buy a few items and look around, Bob Jensen's father was still working behind the meat counter. I went to the cemetery and found the graves of Bob and Carol; someone recently had placed a bouquet of plastic flowers by the girl's headstone.

The account of how the Jensen and King families spent the evening of January 27, 1958, when Bob Jensen and Carol King were murdered, is from newspaper accounts and trial testimony.

The contents of Bob Jensen's billfold were among the boxes of exhibits now in the Clerk of District Court's office at the Lincoln City–County Building.

Additional police photos were shown to me by Sheriff Merle Karnopp.

"Wheels on Fire," by Michael Lydon, appeared in the paperback anthology, US, published by Bantam Books.

In this chapter I made use of autopsy reports, news sources, interviews, statements, and trial transcripts already mentioned.

Chapter Five

I was struck with how virtually every person I interviewed or spoke with informally in and around Lincoln remembered exactly what they were doing at the peak of the murder spree, when the bodies at the Ward residence were found. As long ago as it happened, the Starkweather-Fugate case is still very much on the minds of the people who survived it. The terror they experienced no doubt will never be forgotten. This might, in part, account for the fervor with which some local citizens fight against the release of Caril Fugate.

In this chapter I made use of a telephone interview with Dr. E. D. Zeman, who performed a number of the autopsies.

Some information about the mood of Lincoln during the murder spree was obtained from Gilbert M. Savery, assistant managing editor of the Lincoln *Journal*.

"Badlands Revisited," by Marilyn Coffey, appeared in *The Atlantic Monthly*, December 1974.

I also made use of interviews, news sources, statements, and trial transcripts already mentioned.

Chapter Six

Ninette Beaver, of the staff at KMTV in Omaha, did a television interview of Caril Fugate in 1958. In 1972, she helped make the NBC documentary about Caril, "Growing Up in Prison," and more recently she helped author the book *Caril* (Philadelphia: Lippincott, 1974). I spent part of an evening with Ninette at KMTV, viewing film clips from 1958 of the Starkweather-Fugate case. Some of the descriptions of Charlie and Caril in this and other chapters come from that viewing.

I had a long interview with ex-Police Lieutenant Robert Henninger, who got the confession from Charlie in Wyoming and who later helped obtain the longer, formal statements. He said, "If you're ever going to get a confession out of anybody, you've got to give them a thread to hang onto. A lot of them want to talk, but you've got to give them something that makes what they did seem not quite so bad. With Charlie I said, 'You think you're the bad one, but you're not. When it comes to between you and Caril, you don't even come close.'" Certain details from Henninger's notes, which did not appear in Charlie's formal statements, are occasionally used in this book. These details do not in any way alter the meaning of the formal statements, they merely provide more information. For example, the fact that the rugs Charlie gave Velda Bartlett were mounted carpet samples found in a junkyard came from Henninger's notes.

In this chapter I made use of the book *Wyoming*, which was prepared and published by the Wyoming Writers' Program. I also made use of interviews, news sources, statements, and trial transcripts already mentioned.

Chapter Seven

In this chapter I had several interviews with one of Charlie's attorneys, T. Clement (Clem) Gaughan, now Public Defender of Lancaster County, Nebraska. I also referred to the news sources, statements, and trial transcripts already mentioned.

Chapter Eight

Certain information about Charlie's life in prison came from Lincoln *Journal* staff writer, Marjorie Marlette, who spent considerable time during those days with Charlie and his family. Of all the people who helped with this book, Marjorie possibly helped the most. After seventeen years of covering the case and its aftermath, she was invaluable in guiding me to the right people and, in general, making the research so painless.

Mick Rood, then a reporter for the Omaha *Sun*, took me to Swanton, Nebraska, to interview his father-in-law, ex-prison guard Mike Shimerda. Shimerda spent hours trying to find the picture Charlie gave him just before the execution, but never located it.

I also interviewed John Greenholtz, who was Acting Warden of the Nebraska State Penitentiary at the time of Charlie's execution. Today, he is chairman of the Nebraska Parole Board.

I wish to express thanks to authorities at the Nebraska State Penitentiary — particularly staff member Albert Nance — for allowing me to visit Charlie's cell, retrace the death walk, take photos, and even sit in the electric chair. It was a chilling experience for me, but after so many years of not being used, the chair seems to have lost some of its horror to those around it — as the coffee stain on its arm suggests.

I might mention that there is some dispute over Charlie's actual last words. Most reports are that he said nothing in the execution chamber, that his last words were spoken in his cell: "What's your hurry?" One report, however, is that he said something in the chair about the straps needing to be tightened on his arm.

For an account of the execution, I interviewed Leo Scherer, then a Lincoln *Journal* staff writer who witnessed Charlie's death. Over the years, Scherer has written a number of magazine articles about the experience.

Epilogue

I wish to express thanks to Caril Fugate for visiting with me and to York supervisor Jackie Crawford for helping to arrange the meetings. My meetings with Caril were not interviews — she doesn't consent to them now — but rather visits. In respect to her wishes, I have not quoted her directly, and any information used here which may have passed between us was also gathered from other sources. I talked to a number of people at York about Caril, people in positions of authority who have known her over the years, and was impressed by their unqualified high opinion of her. Recently, I had the pleasure of a visit from Jackie Crawford and Ninette Beaver, who brought me up to date on Caril's activities and state of mind.

For information about Caril's early years in prison, I made use of the book *Caril*, by Ninette Beaver, B. K. Ripley, and Patrick Trese.